# KNOWLEDGE

## The Root of All HAPPINESS

M.A. RISSO

The Book Guild Ltd

First published in Great Britain in 2017 by
The Book Guild Ltd
9 Priory Business Park
Wistow Road, Kibworth
Leicestershire, LE8 0RX
Freephone: 0800 999 2982
www.bookguild.co.uk
Email: info@bookguild.co.uk
Twitter: @bookguild

Copyright © 2017 M. A. Risso

The right of M.A. Risso to be identified as the author of this
work has been asserted by him in accordance with the
Copyright, Design and Patents Act 1988.

All rights reserved. No part of this publication may be
reproduced, transmitted, or stored in a retrieval system, in any form or by any means,
without permission in writing from the publisher, nor be otherwise circulated in
any form of binding or cover other than that in which it is published and without
a similar condition being imposed on the subsequent purchaser.

Typeset in Minion Pro

Printed and bound in Great Britain by CPI Group (UK) Ltd, Croydon, CR0 4YY

ISBN 978 1912083 886

British Library Cataloguing in Publication Data.
A catalogue record for this book is available from the British Library.

# CONTENTS

| | |
|---|---|
| Introduction | vii |
| 1. What Is The Nature Of The Universe? | 1 |
| 2. Who Are We? | 19 |
| 3. Where Do We Come From? | 51 |
| 4. What Is The Goal Of Life? | 69 |
| 5. How Should We Live? | 95 |

# INTRODUCTION

This book is about the fundamental principles of life. It deals with the big questions many of us ask at some point in our lives, such as 'What is the nature of the universe?', 'Who are we?', 'Where do we come from?', 'What is the goal of life?' and 'How should we live?' This book is essentially a book of philosophy. However, unlike many other books of philosophy, it does not use complex language or deal with complex concepts; rather, it deals with the fundamental principles of life in a way that most people should be able to comprehend.

This book is designed to be read by everyone regardless of religion, culture or scientific opinion. It cuts across religious and cultural beliefs and contemplates the truths that lie at the heart of everything we experience and do. Whilst the views contained herein may have much in common with science, religion and other philosophies, this book is not meant to be a commentary on or to expound any other school of thought.

Everybody has a right to their own beliefs in life and a right to express those beliefs. Yet, whilst we may not always agree with the views of others, we should at least accept that everybody is entitled to their own opinions, provided those opinions are not expressed as actions that encroach on other people's rights. Arguably, all humans possess free will, and although our options in life may be restricted by circumstance, if we possess the ability to think freely, we have the chance to explore the nature of the universe and the meaning of life, if we choose to do so.

Science and religion are often at loggerheads, but they do not need to be. With our limited senses, it is simply not possible for humans to understand everything in life and we should have the humility to admit this. However, if we are to make a sincere attempt at trying to understand the nature of the universe and the meaning of life, we should approach it from as many angles as possible. It is extremely shortsighted to try and understand every aspect of life through the disciplines of science, and faith is no longer deemed credible by many unless it can be backed up either with evidence or some very strong logic. Science and religion often disagree because instead of taking the time to understand each other's viewpoints, they spend much of their time and energy defending their own theories. Maybe it's time for science and religion to listen to each other, work together and keep an open mind, and they may then find that life is more than either just physical laws or blind faith.

Finally, this book is purposely short and concise, and

whilst it touches on many widely known and accepted theories, it deliberately avoids discussing specific scientific theories, religious beliefs or philosophies in any great detail. It is very difficult to divorce ourselves from the conditioning of history and culture. Therefore, this book is not intended to be a lengthy and rigorous presentation on what has gone before, but a simple and thought-provoking work that inspires the reader to take a fresh look at life, and attempt to gain knowledge based on an open-minded and logical process. Hopefully, this book will provide the reader with assistance in paving the way to knowledge and happiness.

# 1

# WHAT IS THE NATURE OF THE UNIVERSE?

Any explanation on the nature of the universe that doesn't incorporate some basic scientific principles, specifically the laws of physics, would be incomplete. Similarly, any explanation on the nature of the universe that doesn't incorporate metaphysics would also be incomplete. Whilst physics essentially attempts to explain the mechanics of the universe, such as the nature of matter, energy and their interactions, it doesn't adequately deal with the subtler issues of mind, consciousness and the basis of existence, which are normally dealt with by metaphysics. In order to obtain a broad enough understanding of the nature of the universe, we must look at the physical universe along with the multitude of conscious living beings that occupy and interact with it.

However, before we attempt any explanation on the nature of the universe, we must start at the very beginning and firmly establish three important and seemingly obvious facts, without which the rest of what follows will have no basis.

## I EXIST

'I think, therefore I am'[1] – I may not fully understand who or what I am, but because I possess consciousness, I know I exist.

## THE UNIVERSE EXISTS

I experience an objective reality, therefore the universe exists – I may not fully understand the universe, or even perceive it correctly, but because I experience a reality external to myself, the universe exists.

## TRUTH EXISTS

Because I and the universe exist, truth exists – I may not know the whole truth, but I can conclude that truth must exist because the opposite statement 'truth does not exist' is a contradiction. By saying 'truth does not exist', we must inevitably conclude the statement itself to be untrue, in which case we can immediately dismiss it.

Scientific laws are laws that generally describe a range of

---

1   René Descartes, *Discourse on the Method.*

phenomena based on empirical evidence and can often be proved mathematically, whereas scientific theory often employs only non-empirical methods in order to explain something. However, scientists are increasingly pushing the boundaries of scientific theory to explain a range of phenomena based on theoretical frameworks rather than hard evidence. Whilst pushing the boundaries of scientific theory to explain certain aspects of the universe is, in one sense, admirable, it can also be dangerous and misleading. Theoretical physicists regularly promote their theories with almost religious zeal, often with the hidden goal of gaining recognition. In fact, where science criticises religion and philosophy for being unable to prove their theories with empirical evidence, science, and especially theoretical physics, is doing precisely that. It is putting forward theories based on theoretical frameworks that are not only unproven, but are also sometimes presented in misleading ways. A good example of this is quantum field theory, where some physicists propound the idea that the universe expanded from a quantum vacuum. Now, in principle, there is nothing wrong with putting forward such a theory if it is clearly explained. However, when certain well-known physicists go on to say that this equates to the universe coming into being from nothing, when the quantum vacuum is not truly 'nothing', then this is a misuse of language and quite clearly misleading. As many physicists vigorously promote their unproven theories in much the same way as religion does, one has to question if science is really any better than religion in this respect.

Genuine science and philosophy only ever seek

the truth in whichever field they operate. Any search for knowledge that is tainted by self-promotion, the desire to reinforce one's personal beliefs or for any other reason, is arguably flawed. If a person is simply searching for evidence to justify their own beliefs and lifestyle, it is almost inevitable that the conclusion of that search will be subjective opinion rather than objective knowledge. Religious people are often criticised for being unscientific, and whilst this may be true, it is not entirely fair, as religion attempts to explain that which is not quantifiable by current scientific means. Many religious people and philosophers throughout history, however, have made a sincere and noble effort at trying to answer the fundamental questions of life. Whether we agree with their conclusions or not, we shouldn't doubt that they had the same thirst for knowledge as we do today. In modern times, scientists are often put on a pedestal and promoted as the new true representatives of knowledge. However, whilst it is true that many scientists have made incredible discoveries, scientists do not always act with integrity, they are not always motivated by the best intentions, and their discoveries do not always lead to a better life. Critics of religion may say that religion created God, but critics of science could say it was science that ultimately lead to the creation of the nuclear bomb… You decide which has the greatest potential for destruction.

Physical cosmology is the study of the universe at its largest scale and attempts to explain its origin, nature, evolution and fate. It may seem ridiculous to think that humans can explain the nature of the universe when we can only observe such a small portion of it, but since ancient times humans have been trying to do precisely that. Since the beginning of the renaissance our knowledge of the universe has greatly increased. From Copernicus to Galileo, from Newton to Einstein, along with many other great physicists, mathematicians and astronomers, our understanding of the universe has been completely transformed. Technology, and especially microscopes and telescopes, have been instrumental in improving our understanding of the universe, and modern telescopes are now so powerful that they can detect galaxies that are billions of light years away. However, even though our knowledge of the observable universe has greatly increased, it is debatable whether science is actually much further forward in explaining some of the most fundamental aspects of the universe, such as the nature of life and consciousness. In order to have a balanced theory of the universe, the nature of life and consciousness should also be explored as they are imminent aspects of our day-to-day life, and are no less important.

When trying to establish any theory, we must have an approach that is robust and explores the subject matter from as many angles as possible. We must also try to be as free from conditioning as possible. Throughout life we accumulate layer after layer of conditioning and we view and judge the world through those layers. However, our conditioning is often based on emotion rather than objective knowledge and, therefore, is not always reliable. The universe is an objective reality and certain aspects of its nature can be logically demonstrated. The following are some basic fundamental scientific principles explaining the nature of the universe.

**SOMETHING CANNOT BE CREATED FROM NOTHING**

The laws of physics state that something cannot be created from nothing. In fact, this is not just a law of physics, but is basic logic. You do not need to observe this; in a way, you cannot observe this. However, it can be demonstrated mathematically: $0 + 0 = 0$. It can never = 1 or any other number. The consequence of this is that, regardless of whether the universe had a beginning or not, the sum total of everything that exists has always existed and can never be added to. It can be divided and it can be modified, but the sum total cannot be increased.

**SOMETHING CANNOT BE REDUCED TO NOTHING**

Just as something cannot be created from nothing, so something cannot be reduced to nothing… at least, not absolute nothing. The consequence of this is that the sum total of everything that exists will always exist and can never be completely destroyed. It can be divided and it can be modified, but the sum total cannot be reduced to nothing.

**THINGS CAN ONLY BE MODIFIED AND NOT COMPLETELY DESTROYED**

Although the sum total of everything that exists has always existed and cannot be reduced to nothing, some people will still argue that things can be destroyed. Whilst it is true that things can be destroyed, you can never actually get rid of the matter or energy that an object is comprised of. For example, you may cut something into the smallest pieces, but you have only destroyed its structural integrity – the pieces still exist. Or, you may burn something, but again you have only destroyed its structural integrity, as the substances, compounds, elements and particles have simply been dissipated or modified. We can go on with lots of other examples, but the point is that everything within existence can only ever be modified and never completely destroyed.

## THERE IS NO SUCH THING AS NOTHING

Nothing does not exist because, by definition, nothing is nonexistent, it is 'no thing'. In fact, just by speaking or writing about nothing is, in a way, a contradiction, and we can only speak or write about nothing as an abstract concept.

The conclusion of the above scientific principles is that the sum total of everything that exists has always existed and will always exist;[2] and, whilst things appear to be destroyed, they are, in fact, only ever divided, dissipated and modified. This conclusion is, in a sense, quite comforting, because it establishes that existence in whatever form is actually eternal. However, although

---

[2] Care must be taken here not to equate the universe with the sum total of existence.

existence is eternal, the universe is quite clearly changing and everything is affected by different forces of attraction and repulsion. We may not fully understand the forces at play in the universe, nevertheless, science generally accepts that there are four fundamental forces affecting everything: gravitational, electromagnetic, strong nuclear and weak nuclear. Even if we don't understand how these forces work on a scientific level, the important thing is to know that such forces exist, and they affect everything we experience and do. From the way atoms behave, to how the universe was formed, the forces of attraction and repulsion can be seen everywhere.

But why is this relevant to our understanding of the nature of the universe? Well, it is relevant because not only do these forces affect our lives on a physical level, but the forces of attraction and repulsion also affect us on a metaphysical level. Our minds are constantly being controlled by an attraction to one thing and a repulsion to another, and we are constantly making decisions on whether we want to connect and engage with certain aspects of the universe or not, whilst being driven on by a desire to be fulfilled. Of course, this can partly be explained by our biological make-up, but it also calls into question the nature of consciousness and its place in the universe. Although the forces of attraction and repulsion are responsible for an ever-changing universe, they do not detract from the fact that the sum total of everything that exists is eternal.

Now we have established that existence is eternal, we should next address the question of whether there is a principal source for the universe, if it has multiple sources, or if it does not have a source at all, but instead just exists as it does now, albeit constantly changing. This is not so easy to answer, and whilst there are scientific theories regarding this, in reality they are hard to prove beyond all doubt. Currently, the most widely accepted scientific theory regarding the origin of the universe is the Big Bang theory. The Big Bang theory basically states that around 14 billion years ago, the universe expanded from a singularity to create the universe we see today. This expansion continues, and scientists claim there is evidence of this in the existence of microwave background radiation and redshift (when light moves away from the observer, the wavelength of the observed light appears longer and it moves towards the red end of the spectrum, which is called redshift). Although the Big Bang theory is currently the most widely accepted scientific theory regarding the origin of the universe, the theory is not without its critics.

Some scientists believe that the universe may have multiple sources, or even that it has been previously created only to be retracted back to its source again, and the whole process of creation and retraction has occurred many times before. Some also believe that it is possible the universe has always existed in some form or another, but is in a constant state of flux. Or, even that there are other universes and dimensions that our limited senses are physically incapable of detecting. However, although we don't fully understand how or when the universe came into existence, the scientific evidence to suggest that the universe does have a beginning is overwhelming. And, because the universe exists within measurable space and time, it also does not seem logically valid that the universe is infinite and that it has an infinite number of previous events – a further reason to believe the universe has a beginning. Also, because something cannot come from nothing, if the universe does have a beginning, we must therefore conclude that it has a cause.[3] Of course, humans are merely tiny beings in a phenomenally large universe, and we can only perceive what our limited senses allow us to perceive. However, in one sense, it is unimportant how or when the universe came into being, because it does not change the fact that the sum total of everything that exists has always existed, and will always exist.

The creation of the universe from a single source is a theory that many religions and science agree with. Most monotheistic and monistic religions believe that God, and only God, created the universe and everything within it; however, this belief in a single source of the universe is often where any similarities between science and religion ends. Whilst some scientists do believe in God as the principal source of the universe, many don't, and there is also general disagreement between science and religion as to what happened after the initial creation, or Big Bang. In a way, what happened after is academic, as humans must accept that they cannot possibly understand everything about the universe. However, the fact that science, many religions and philosophies agree on the theory that the universe originated from a single

---

[3] For a simple but compelling argument on this, see The Kalam Cosmological Argument as propounded by William Lane Craig.

source is remarkable common ground. Maybe it's time for science, religion and philosophy to come together and recognise what they have in common rather than what separates them.

Another aspect of the universe that should be explored is space and time. We say 'aspect' because it is often thought that space and time are intrinsically linked, and it has been argued by many that one cannot exist without the other. The existence of space and time may seem obvious, but scientists and philosophers throughout the ages have pondered whether either actually exist independently of the mind at all. Another reason for questioning the nature of space and time is that, when a person experiences the world around them, they actually experience it as a continuum. A person may experience different objects and dimensions that give the appearance of space and time, but they still experience the world as a continuum. For thousands of years, humans have tried to create ways of measuring time, and we currently measure so-called time in seconds, minutes, hours, days, etc. As we move through the seasons and years, our experiences create a host of impressions on the mind that we often choose to recall through the capacity of the memory. The strange thing about the past is that it actually doesn't exist, other than as a memory which we can only experience in the present. Similarly, the future also doesn't exist, other than as a thought that we experience in the mind during the present. In fact, only the present ever exists.

We previously stated that it is often thought that space and time are intrinsically linked. We can demonstrate this with the following example: if upon being born we had no senses or bodily functions whatsoever other than uninterrupted sight and a brain, and let's also assume we had sufficient nourishment to keep the body going for many years without the requirement for it to be moved. When we are born we are immediately placed in front of a blank white screen, and that white screen is consistently white all over, with no visible edges or shadows; all we can see is a pure white screen. We sit in front of the white screen for many years not being able to move or sense any other aspect of the world. Now, in the absence of any other sensory perception, we would have no concept of space or time, as we can only experience a single continuous dimension, namely the white screen. Let's suppose that after many years of being in front of the white screen, a black line appears down the middle; all of a sudden, both space and time have been created simultaneously. Space has been created because a new dimension has been introduced in the form of the black line boundary, and time has been created because now the observer has a pre-black line period and a post-black line period.

The conclusion of the above is that both space and time exist as a continuum and have no beginning or end, only the present exists, and we can only have a concept of space and time if the universe is multi-dimensional, which it is. This conclusion ties in nicely with the previous conclusion that existence is eternal.

We have now looked at some key scientific principles relating to the nature of the physical universe, albeit at a basic level, and we've even briefly mentioned the concept of space and time and how it is perceived. We will now consider the subtler nature of life and consciousness. Life and consciousness are essentially one and the same thing and, as already mentioned, is a subject that is normally dealt with by metaphysics. However, physicists are increasingly looking at this subject within the field of quantum mechanics. Whilst cosmology is the science that studies the nature of the universe at its largest scale, quantum mechanics generally studies the nature of things at their smallest scale – nanoparticles, atoms, subatomic particles and their interactions. Whether studying the universe at its largest or smallest scale, science has for many years had the niggling problem of the nature of consciousness. It has been a problem because, whilst scientists acknowledge consciousness exists, they have struggled to explain what it is and how it exists. Recently, physicists have developed theories to try and explain consciousness within the context of quantum theory; however, there is currently much debate within science as to the validity of those theories. Philosophy and religion has not been shy in attempting to explain the nature of consciousness; in fact, it has been one of the subject matters that has dominated philosophy and religion for thousands of years, and continues to do so today.

So, what is the problem of consciousness? Well, the main problem is trying to explain what it is and how it arises. Is consciousness something that is independent of the body and eternal, or is it something that is created by the body and dies when the body dies? In order to attempt to answer this question, we must first clearly establish what consciousness is. Consciousness is ultimately the observer, the thing that experiences the external world. Consciousness is not any of the senses, or even the brain; it is the final observer. Whilst our senses are the instruments that gather information about the external world, and our brain is the organ that processes that information, neither the senses nor the brain actually observe anything. Also, the electrochemical signals within the brain are just that and nothing else; they are not the final observer, but the thing that is observed or experienced. Consciousness is not even the process of thought, or the accumulation of experiences that we call the mind; again, it is just the observer, or the one that experiences thought. If one day we were to lose our sight or any of our other senses, the conscious observer wouldn't have actually changed, only what we are able to observe and experience would have changed. In the same way, if one day we were unfortunate enough to lose all of our senses and were unable to experience anything of the external world, the conscious observer would still exist, we just wouldn't be able to experience anything, other than possibly memory. In fact, the state of being unable to observe or experience anything whatsoever would be like having no consciousness; however, in reality consciousness is still there as the 'consciousness principal',[4] with the potential to experience as soon as an external reality is available to it. From a scientific point of view, it may seem odd to divide consciousness in this way. Many neuroscientists postulate that consciousness

---

4   In the context of consciousness, I take the word 'Principal' to mean 'First'. Also, not to be confused with 'Principle'.

simply arises as a result of brain activity; however, although brain activity creates experience, it doesn't really explain the nature of subjectivity or the desire for life.

If, then, consciousness is purely the subjective observer that becomes active as soon as it experiences the objective world, how does it come about? Interestingly, consciousness is present in all creatures and, arguably, in all living things, although until fairly recently science hadn't seriously considered this a possibility. The only thing that makes consciousness seem different in different creatures is not the consciousness principal itself, but the nature of the senses that each individual creature possesses and the way it processes information. A good example of this are bats. Bats, along with some other animals, use echolocation, a sense or ability that humans do not possess. Now, we may understand how echolocation works, and we may even understand how bats process echolocation information, but we cannot really have an accurate understanding of how echolocation is perceived by bats if we do not possess this ability ourselves. We could use many other examples of creatures that have very different bodies and senses to humans, and whilst they may perceive the world differently, the consciousness principal is the same in all of them, and still acts as the final observer. Another way we can demonstrate the nature of consciousness is through sleep. When we are in deep sleep, it appears that we are no longer conscious, as our senses have, in a way, shut down. However, just because we are unaware of the world around us during deep sleep, it does not mean we have no consciousness; rather, it means our consciousness is not registering the outside world, and we are, therefore, not even aware of our own consciousness. This clearly demonstrates that in order to experience consciousness, it requires both an observer and an external stimulus, and without an external stimulus, whilst the consciousness principal still exists, we cannot recognise it as such.

If, then, there are many different types of creatures but the same consciousness principal present in all of them, how can consciousness be created by the body? How can such different bodies as humans and insects, for example, create the same consciousness principal? Well, the reality is, they don't. Consciousness is a potential that is not created by the body but is limited by the body, and is the consistent subjective principal that only appears to come into being when it comes into contact with the objective world. Also, because consciousness is not subject to the general laws of science, it cannot be divided, dissipated or modified by any physical process. It only appears to be modified or conditioned through experience.

In the above, we may have defined consciousness, but we still haven't really explained if, and how, the consciousness principal arises. However, this is not something that is easy to establish, and if we could, then we would have solved one of life's greatest mysteries. Maybe for now we should be content with the knowledge that because consciousness does exist, it must always exist, either as the principal observer that we have already defined, as a possibility, or in some other mode. We can come to this conclusion because even if consciousness is a creation or manifestation of matter and energy, we have already established that the sum total of everything that exists is eternal. Therefore, if consciousness is somehow created or manifest, it cannot be greater than its source, which would mean that, ultimately, consciousness in an even greater form or mode must exist within its source, namely matter or energy. It is, of course, very possible (and many would argue very probable) that the opposite is actually true, and consciousness is the basis of existence and the origin of everything in the universe, including individual consciousness. As the German theoretical physicist Max Planck once said, 'I regard consciousness as fundamental. I regard matter as derivative from consciousness. We cannot get behind consciousness. Everything that we talk about, everything that we regard as existing, postulates consciousness.'[5]

In respect of our first question 'What is the nature of the universe?', we can summarise our findings as follows:

**Existence is eternal, and although it may be difficult to firmly establish if the universe has a single source, multiple sources, or eternally exists in a constant state of flux, the sum total of everything cannot be decreased or increased, just modified.**

**Everything in the universe is affected by different forces of attraction and repulsion. Because these forces act on both a physical and metaphysical level, it calls into question the nature of consciousness and its place in the universe.**

---

5   *The Observer* (25 January 1931).

Space and time have no beginning or end, and it is only the perception of a multi-dimensional world that makes us think that space and time can be measured.

Life and consciousness are also eternal, and whilst it is difficult to firmly establish if life and consciousness are a manifestation of matter and energy, or if matter and energy are a manifestation of life and consciousness, ultimately it is of no consequence, as one must exist as a potential in the other for either to exist.

# 2

# WHO ARE WE?

When trying to understand who we are, we should once again use both a scientific and metaphysical approach, as when we refer to the individual self, we generally refer to a combination of the physical body, mind and conscious life force working together as a single being. From a biological point of view, humans are simply animals; however, many people believe that humans are uniquely intelligent and are in some way superior to other animals. Whilst this may or may not be true, we are nevertheless just animals. The field of biology divides all life into taxonomic ranks, the first rank being Kingdom (or Domain, depending on the system used). A kingdom is a taxonomic rank that divides different life forms into groups on the basis that their common characteristics suggest they are descendants of a common ancestor. Whilst there are different kingdom systems being used in different parts of the world, one of the most common systems currently being used is the Five Kingdom System. Each kingdom is divided into Phyla and each Phylum is further divided into Classes. Under each Class, there are further subdivisions: Order, Family, Genus and Species. Because we are still learning about the natural world, the definition and number of taxonomic groups is constantly changing. The following is a very brief description of the different kingdoms based on the commonly used, but often disputed, Five Kingdom System.

### ANIMALIA

Consisting of all animals in approximately 35 phyla, of which there are around 10 main phyla. Humans are mammals within the chordate phylum.

### PLANTAE

Consisting of all plants in a generally accepted 12 phyla.

### FUNGI

Consisting of all fungi, including moulds and yeasts, with between 3 and 7 generally accepted phyla.

### PROTISTA

A diverse group of organisms, often with little in common and comprising of at least 16 phyla. Some share animal characteristics, some fungi and some have plant characteristics such as the algae and seaweeds.

**MONERA**

Different types of bacteria including blue-green algae. Some consider this an outdated kingdom with an undetermined number of phyla.

The diversity and number of life forms inhabiting the earth is truly incredible, and the fact that humans are still discovering new species just goes to show how incomplete our knowledge is. Other than obvious physical characteristics, it can be difficult to understand what makes humans similar to other life forms and what makes them different. We may look at our biological make-up and see similarities with other creatures, but how much does that really tell us about ourselves and what we have in common with other life forms?

In order to understand who we are, we also need to look at our behaviour and compare it with the behaviour of other life forms. There are some basic behaviours that we share with all animals, and even some behaviours we share with all life forms. For example, with all animals we share the requirement to feed, defend, rest and procreate in order to maintain life and to produce new life. And, with all other life forms we at least share the requirement to feed and procreate/multiply, although it could be argued that with certain other life forms, especially some plants, we also share the requirement to defend and rest.[1] It is in one sense remarkable that we share so much common behaviour with other life forms when they appear to be so different from us, but in another sense it is not surprising, as we share so much of our genetic make-up. What this goes to show is that whilst different life forms may have different feeding, defending, resting and procreating habits, they all share the same underlying desire to live. This desire to live, regardless of how small, is only ever quashed when life has become so unfulfilling or painful that it is more desirable to end life. The desire to end life is arguably not only found in humans, but in some animals too. Although in nature there are a number of examples of animals that appear to voluntarily end their lives, most of these cases can be explained as something other than a desire to end life.[2] However, there are numerous documented cases of animals that have appeared to grieve or suffer from extreme anxiety, which has resulted in either self-destructive behavior, or a complete lack of desire for life. This demonstrates that whether you are a human or any other living being, the fact that we share the desire to feed and procreate, and even the desire to defend and rest, means that all living beings are primarily driven by the fundamental desire to live. It is not, however, just a desire to live that drives us. As mentioned, if life is unfulfilling or painful, then the desire to live greatly decreases; therefore, we can conclude that all living beings are ultimately driven

---

1 Not only do many plants become dormant during winter, but they also have a day and night cycle (Circadian Rhythm).

2 For example, some varieties of carpenter ants explode as a defence mechanism.

by the desire to live in happiness, and to just exist is not enough.

When we talk about happiness, we are really referring to a state of consciousness and sense of wellbeing that is experienced when one is fulfilled. Interestingly, in nature all of the basic activities we have to perform in order to live, such as eating, mating and sleeping, also provide a great deal of fulfilment and happiness. As for defending, we only do this when we recognise that we may lose our facility for life and happiness, even if this relates to loss of territory or way of life. For most people and other animals, eating is a great pleasure, mating is a great pleasure and sleeping is, in a way, enjoyable, as it refreshes the body in order to once again enjoy life to its fullest. In fact, if these activities were not pleasurable, we may have died out a long time ago. If the requirement to eat had no pleasure attached to it, how healthy would we be and how long would we live? Similarly, if mating wasn't a pleasure, how long would the human race or any other species exist? Humans, and arguably all living beings, are motivated to act out of a desire for fulfilment or happiness. Other living beings may not have the same level of consciousness or feel happiness in quite the same way as humans do, but every living being will have a kind of fulfilment according to its own nature.

In the same way that science has been very slow to explore the nature of consciousness, science has also been extremely slow to recognise that animals are conscious beings that possess emotions, and that along with other living beings, are motivated by the desire for life and happiness. These are areas that science has only recently began to look into in any seriousness. For years we have been told that animals have no or little consciousness and possess no or few emotions. This is complete folly as scientists acknowledge that we share much of our genetic make-up with other animals. They also acknowledge them as living creatures that need to eat, mate, sleep and defend. So, why have they been so slow to recognise that they may also possess consciousness and emotions similar to humans? Anyone who has ever owned a pet would have observed that animals display emotions. They display feelings of happiness, excitement, aggression, fear and anxiety, as well as other complex emotions. Many animals are social creatures, and when left alone for long periods of time, they become anxious or display symptoms of depression. Animals also act out of a desire for happiness. They often show a preference for certain types of food, they engage in sexual acts purely for pleasure and they perform many other activities simply because they enjoy doing them, and not always out of necessity.[3] Even from a biological point of view, the vast majority of animals have sense receptors, and most have a brain and nervous system. And even those animals that don't have a brain and nervous system, will still normally have some form of decentralised nervous system. After many years, scientists are finally starting to recognise that animals do, in fact, possess consciousness, feel pleasure and pain, and also possess emotions similar to humans. The body of evidence suggesting this is so great

---

[3] Marc Bekoff, former Professor of Ecology and Evolutionary Biology at the University of Colorado, has written extensively on this subject.

that science can no longer ignore the obvious, even if it does not fit comfortably with their long-held theories.

We have so far established that humans are a combination of the physical body, mind and conscious life force working together as a single being. We have also established that humans are a species that have much in common with other life forms, both on a biological level and on many other levels. Finally, we have established that the underlying motivation for human and animal activity is the desire for life and happiness. We will now demonstrate in greater detail how all human activity is motivated by this desire for life and happiness.

As already mentioned, the primary functions that promote and sustain life are eating, mating, defending and sleeping. Not only do these functions promote and sustain life, but they also promote happiness. However, receiving an education, having a certain occupation, living in a house, driving a car, going on holiday, participating in sports, enjoying consumer products and many other activities are all undertaken with the ultimate objective of promoting life and happiness. Some activities do not obviously appear to be undertaken with the desire to promote life and happiness; however, if you analyse the primary reason why those activities are undertaken, the root desire is always to promote life and happiness. A good example of this is education, which, whilst the process of studying itself may not always be enjoyable, we engage in this activity with the ultimate objective to improve life and become happier. Another example is war, which again, whilst the activity itself is not normally considered to be enjoyable, it is something that, rightly or wrongly, we decide to engage in to protect and promote life and happiness.

Humans undertake many other activities that do not directly provide much happiness, or appear to directly promote life, but are, in a sense, sacrificial activities that are driven by the final objective of life and happiness. Even religion is no different. Whilst those who follow a religion may get a great deal of happiness and comfort from following it, there are certain sacrificial religious practices that do not appear to be very enjoyable, such as refraining from certain activities and following various disciplines. However, just like the person who studies hard for many years, the ultimate objective of the religious person is also life and happiness… even if it is believed that most of the fruits of such activities are enjoyed in a next life. We do not need to provide other examples, although a good exercise to perform whenever we undertake any activity is to ask ourselves 'What is the primary reason why I am performing this activity?' Whilst the primary reason is not always immediately obvious, if you dig deep enough for the answer, that answer will always be the desire for life and happiness.

Although we have clearly demonstrated that the desire for life and happiness is the motivation that underpins and drives all human activity, we should also very briefly look at the nature of fear. Fear is, in a way, the extreme opposite of desire; however, both feelings are intrinsically connected. In fact, desire and fear are essentially just two sides of the same coin, because fear is actually the concern that we may lose life and happiness, or at least, some aspect of it, and instead feel pain or loss.

It could be said that our desires drive us forward in life and our fears hold us back.

As we move through life and have different experiences, we build up an ever changing picture of the world. Sometimes those experiences make us happy and sometimes they make us sad. Sometimes, after experiencing the same thing numerous times, we may recognise good or bad qualities that we never noticed before, and as a result, our opinions change. An example of this is going on holiday. We go on holiday to a different country with high expectations, but when we arrive there is a delay at the hotel check-in, days of bad weather, the resort appears dirty, and to top things off, we get sick. We may return from that holiday with the irrational belief that it was not a nice country, our view being completely tainted by our poor experience. Years later, we return to the same country, but to a different hotel and resort. This time, the hotel check-in is efficient, the hotel and resort are beautiful, we have two weeks of hot sunny weather and experience perfect health throughout. All of a sudden, our opinion of the country changes and we put the first holiday down to bad luck. This kind of scenario is being played out in so many areas of our life, and our opinions often change and develop through repeated experience.

If, then, we naturally make judgements on whether something is good or bad through experience, what is it precisely that makes something good or bad? What is the definition of good and bad? This may seem like an odd question to ask, as every day we automatically make decisions on whether something is good or bad with little thought. But actually, this is another question that philosophy and religion has been asking for thousands of years. The main problem being, is good and bad something that is subjective opinion based on personal taste, or is it something that is objective truth based on some consistent principle? We can tackle this question in two ways. For the first way, we will use the example of a common object; it can be any object, but we will use the example of a chair. Now, a chair's primary function is to provide convenient rest for the body by being sat on. However, if a chair is uncomfortable, has uneven legs, and does not provide the correct support for the body, then we consider the chair to be a bad chair on the basis that it does not perform its primary function very well. If, however, a chair is comfortable, has even legs and provides the correct support for the body, we say it is a good chair. Can we then safely conclude that something is either good or bad based on how well it performs its primary function? Well, no, and we can use another example to demonstrate this. A bomb's primary function is to cause destruction, and we may create a bomb that causes a huge amount of destruction. Now, a bomb is a good bomb if it performs its primary function to destroy well; however, many people would argue that the bomb was not good at all, but bad. This demonstrates that on one level, something is 'relatively' good only in so far as how well it performs its intended function, but it doesn't mean it is ultimately good.

We will now go back to our example of the chair. Let's suppose that we have two chairs; they are both as comfortable as each other, they both have even legs and they both provide equally good support for the body. However, one of the chairs is very plain looking and has chipped paint, whilst the other one has very beautiful carvings on it and is nicely varnished. Now, the carvings and varnish do not add anything to the chair's ability to perform its primary function, but because it is more beautiful, we consider it to be a good or better chair.

For the second way of tackling the definition of good and bad, instead of looking at how well something performs its primary function, we will examine what something's ultimate purpose is in order to define whether it is good or bad. Again, we can use our example of the chair. We have already stated that the purpose of the chair is to provide convenient rest for the body. We also know that sometimes the body requires rest in order for it to function properly, and if we never rested our bodies, we would compromise our quality of life. Therefore, although the chair is designed to perform a specific function, its ultimate purpose is really to promote life and happiness, and it is for this reason that we consider the chair to be good. We consider a chair to be bad because, if it does not adequately perform its primary function to provide proper support and rest for the body, then it does not promote life and happiness very well. This, then, is really the key to establishing whether something is good or bad – not just whether it performs its intended function, but its ability to promote life and happiness. This is why our more beautiful chair is better, because it promotes life and happiness both through its ability to perform its intended function, and because it is more visually pleasing. This is also why that, although our bomb may perform its intended function well, because its ultimate purpose is to cause destruction, many people would not consider it to be good. We can take this principle further and apply it to all aspects of life. We do not just attribute the concept of good and bad to objects, but also to thoughts and actions. We consider those thoughts and actions to be good when they are likely to promote life and happiness, e.g. thoughts and acts of love and kindness towards others, respect for oneself, exercising, or eating a healthy diet. Those thoughts and actions that promote destruction and misery, we consider to be bad.

We can conclude from the above that, although due to experience people have different subjective opinions on whether something is good or bad, we can, however, say that the actual definition of good and bad is an objective and consistent principle – the definition of good being something that promotes life and happiness, and the definition of bad being something that causes destruction and misery. Once again, a good exercise to perform whenever we decide something is good or bad is to ask ourselves 'What is the primary reason why I think this is good or bad?' If you analyse the real reason, the answer will always be that it is either good because you believe it promotes life and happiness, or it is bad because you believe it causes destruction and misery. We have now established two very important and fundamental principles that help us define who we are: 1) Everything we do in life is motivated by the desire for life and happiness, and 2) We define all things in life as being either good or bad on the basis of their perceived ability to provide life and happiness. This shows that life and happiness are the most fundamental requirements of our being.

Although we have now clearly defined the nature of good and bad, we have previously only briefly touched on why people find certain things good or bad based on experience. There are many things in life that most people accept as being good, such as eating a healthy, balanced diet. Even if the fine details of what constitutes a healthy, balanced diet cannot always be agreed on, most people would agree that, in principle, eating a healthy, balanced diet is good as it promotes life and happiness. However, there are also many things in life where there is a great deal of disagreement as to whether they are good or bad. The reason for this is because in reality, everything in this physical world has elements of good and bad, although some things have more good than bad and vice versa. We can demonstrate this using our previous examples of the chair and the bomb. Previously, we concluded that if a chair performs its primary function to provide convenient rest and support for the body well, which in turn promotes life and happiness, then it must be good. However, that is not the whole story. The chair in itself may be an innocent enough object, but if we also take into consideration the fact that we use large amounts of the world's resources to manufacture chairs, such as trees, metal and oil, and that the processes used in obtaining those resources and making and distributing the chairs cause significant amounts of pollution, then all of a sudden our humble chair doesn't seem quite so good. Also, we could argue that if a chair is too comfortable, then it may promote laziness, which again, many would not consider to be good.

In the same way, previously we concluded that many people would consider a bomb to be bad due to its ability to cause destruction and misery, but again, that is not the whole story. It could be argued that bombs can and have been used for good purposes. An example of this would be where a political leader tries to take over another country by force, with the objective of destroying and violently suppressing innocent people. In this situation, the deployment of bombs along with other instruments of warfare as a deterrent may be considered good. Although initially the bombs may cause a huge amount of destruction and misery, it could be argued that they were used for the greater long-term good of protecting a country's people and its future generations.[4]

Therefore, in order to accurately assess how good or bad something is, we must consider many things, such as what its purpose is, how well it performs its intended function and the short and long-term impact it may have on ourselves, others and the environment. Without considering all of these aspects, we cannot come to an accurate conclusion on how well something promotes life and happiness, and therefore, how good or bad something is. It could be argued that nothing in the observable material world is completely good, as there does not appear to be anything materially that gives eternal life and happiness. In the same way, it could be said that nothing is completely bad, as we have

---

[4] Of course, this would be a highly contentious view.

already concluded that the sum total of everything in the universe cannot be destroyed, just modified. Also, even though all around us we continually witness life coming to an end, we also continually witness new life coming into being.

We have now given a lengthy explanation on the nature of good and bad, and how we ultimately define how good or bad something is according to its ability to promote life and happiness. This explanation was given in order to have a deeper understanding of who we really are and what motivates our thoughts and actions. We can also apply these principles to ourselves, and by doing so, we will see that humans are an ever-changing mixture of good and bad, as sometimes our actions promote life and happiness, and sometimes they cause destruction and misery.

All humans, and indeed, all living beings, are merely products of their genetic make-up and life experience. How much of our behaviour is determined by our genetics, and how much is determined by our experiences and environment, is a debate that has been going on within the field of psychology for many years. The Nature vs. Nurture debate will no doubt continue for many more years, and whilst it may be important to establish whether it is our genetic make-up or our experiences that mainly determine our behaviour, it is not necessarily that important for establishing who we really are. The primary desire that motivates us in life is still the desire for life and happiness, and we thereby judge things as we move through life by this criterion, even if we are not always aware that we are doing so. Our true self is like the driver of a vehicle; the vehicle is the body, and life and happiness is our destination. As the driver, we have a desire to reach our destination, and the body is the vehicle that helps us do so. As we travel, sometimes the journey is enjoyable as we look through the windows of our eyes and see the sunshine and beautiful scenery; at other times we may experience bad weather, or even come across obstacles that cause frustration and slow our progress. Sometimes, after observing our situation and surroundings, we may think we have taken a wrong turn and decide to change course. In fact, as the journey of life is a long one, we may change course many times. During the course of our journey we also have to provide fuel for our bodily vehicle in the form of food, in order for it to move towards its destination. Our bodily vehicle even sometimes breaks down and needs repairing. Through the good and bad experiences of our journey, and following numerous wrong turns and breakdowns, we may come to the conclusion that our ultimate destination of life and happiness does not, in fact, exist. If we come to this conclusion, we will inevitably resign ourselves to just enjoying the ride whilst trying to deal with any bad experiences that come our way. However, although we may come to this conclusion, what we often overlook is that life in the form of the driver exists throughout the course of the journey, and we also witness happiness numerous times throughout too. Therefore, life and happiness must already exist in principle. In other words, sometimes we can become so preoccupied with trying to reach our goal of life and happiness, that we fail to notice that it already exists in the present. Of course, 'complete' life and happiness may not exist in the present, but the fact that it exists in principle should give us faith that our destination does actually exist.

The above analogy is actually a rather crude one, and although it demonstrates a point, it has its limitations in explaining who we are and the nature of our situation. However, what it may make us ask is 'What is the true nature of the self?' We previously concluded that consciousness is the principal that exists as the subjective and final observer, and although it is always present, it only becomes aware of itself when it experiences the objective world. So, is consciousness the true self? Well, yes, but it is only one aspect of the true self, because consciousness on its own is just the ability to be aware and doesn't take into account the motivation for life and happiness. Interestingly, at those points in life when we have a deep sense of fulfilment and when we are at our happiest, we actually lose our desire. During those moments we even lose our sense of fear. Those moments can be rare, but when we experience them, we often cherish them forever. These experiences can be the simplest pleasures when everything in the world seems to be just right, such as enjoying quality time with a loved one, walking on a beautiful beach, sitting in a beautiful garden on a sunny day, or achieving a goal. When we are caught up in those moments, notice how we are happy just to exist in the moment and how we lose all sense of fear and desire. We may briefly have the thought that we don't want the experience to end, but as soon as that brief thought is over, we again become absorbed in the experience and lose all fear and desire. What this goes to show is that desire only exists when we are not fulfilled and happy, and because we are not fulfilled and happy all of the time, we are constantly busy going here and there in the pursuit of happiness. We are often prepared to work long hours in careers we don't always enjoy in the pursuit of happiness. We also make all kinds of other sacrifices on a daily basis in the pursuit of happiness, and it can sometimes be incredible to see what lengths some people will go to in order to obtain the objects of their desires. This shows that we often neglect the simple, good things that promote life and happiness in the present, and spend far too much time being preoccupied with the future, or even dwelling on the past. That doesn't mean we shouldn't remember the past or think about the future, it just means we should have a healthy balance of making the most of life in the present, whilst learning from our past and preparing for the future.

But what about the person who appears to be evil? Why do some people appear to get pleasure from destructive behaviour, or from hurting or even killing others? Strangely, such people are acting out of the same desire for life and happiness as they believe that somehow, their actions will give them some kind of fulfilment; however, they act out of a purely self-centred compulsion born of ignorance. Although it could be argued that everyone's actions are ultimately selfish, there is a difference between good selfish acts which are born out of knowledge, and bad selfish acts which are born out of ignorance.

An example of how good selfish acts arise are ones that start from a desire to be happy, and through a combination of a person's genetic make-up, positive life experience and observations, a person learns they cannot exist alone, and that they are dependent on others and the wider environment for happiness. As they open themselves up to positive experiences such as love, light and beauty, they gain faith in life and become increasingly fulfilled, which in turn creates a great sense of life and happiness. In this situation, desire and fear decreases and a person develops greater knowledge.

An example of how bad selfish acts arise are ones that also start from the same desire to be happy, but due to a combination of a person's genetic make-up, negative life experience and observations, a person feels they want to live isolated from others, and that they are not dependent on others and the wider environment for happiness. As they close themselves off from positive experiences such as love, light and beauty, they lose faith in life and become increasingly unfulfilled, and out of frustration, become angry, destructive or miserable. If a person continues on this path, they become increasingly isolated and frustrated, and will resort to whatever options are available for their gratification. Also, because they become increasingly isolated from others, they may lose any sense of empathy. In this situation, desire and fear increase and a person sinks into ignorance.

We could use less extreme examples, however, the common features in all of them would be a combination of a person's genetic make-up and life experience that either lead to a place of knowledge resulting in happiness, or a place of ignorance resulting in misery. In reality, most, if not all, people have a varying mixture of both at different times. Because people have a mixture of both depending on their situation at any given moment, we are all constantly going back and forth between happiness and misery. This is why people sometimes appear to be good and sometimes appear to be bad. During those moments in life when a person feels fulfilled and happy, they are more likely to display good qualities such as kindness, charity and love.[5] This is because the direction of the subjective self is outward towards the objective world, and connecting with it. Connecting with the objective world, in a way, lights up the subjective conscious self, giving it a sense of fulfilment. During those moments in life when a person feels unfulfilled and miserable, they are less likely to display good qualities, and more likely to display qualities such as selfishness, hatred and envy. This is because the direction of the subjective self is inward towards itself, thereby disconnecting with the objective world. When a person disconnects with the objective world, the subjective conscious self, in a way, becomes darkened and there is a greater sense of being unfulfilled. As previously mentioned, when we become unfulfilled, desire, fear and misery increase and we are less likely to display qualities of kindness, charity and love. This is partly because life becomes so miserable that we lack the energy and motivation to connect with the objective world, and partly because our most pressing

---

5   A number of studies suggest that acts of kindness also promote happiness, including a study by Kathryn Buchanan and Anat Bardi, published in the *Journal of Social Psychology* (Vol. 150, No. 3, 2010, pp. 235-237).

concern is with ourselves. Most people snap out of these negative moments; however, if a person continues in this inwardly selfish direction it can be dangerous, as they may end up in a dark and emotionally destructive place that becomes increasingly difficult to get out of.

Previously, we stated that our life force along with its essential quality of consciousness is eternal, because the sum total of everything that exists is eternal. We also stated that it was ultimately of no consequence whether life and consciousness are a manifestation of matter and energy, or whether matter and energy are a manifestation of life and consciousness, as one must exist as a potential in the other for either to exist. However, in order to fully explain who we are and what our true nature is, we should try to establish if, and how, this conscious life force comes about. Many people believe that the soul or life force is eternal, and many believe that it dies when the body dies. Although it may not currently be possible to empirically prove whether the life force is eternal or not, there are, however, some very strong indicators that suggest it is. Firstly, science states that everything in the universe is made up of energy. Secondly, the law of conservation of energy states that energy is neither created nor destroyed, just transformed and transferred. We know that our life force along with its essential quality of consciousness exists; therefore, life must also be energy, although not necessarily as we know it. In fact, it is not difficult to understand that our conscious life force is energy, as it is the ultimate 'force' that moves the body. Therefore, if our life force is energy, and all energy is eternal, we must also conclude that our life force is eternal. The fact that energy is never destroyed but simply transferred from one thing to another, just goes to show that this energy we call the life force also does not get destroyed upon the body's death, but gets transferred from one body or situation to another.

If life isn't present in the body, the body cannot move. Although the body requires energy in the form of food, it still also requires an animating force that possesses a desire for life and happiness in order for it to move independently. Without a life force, the body is simply an inanimate object. Because we can observe this life force along with its essential quality of consciousness in our own bodies, and if we accept that this life force is inhabiting and animating all kinds of living beings, we must therefore conclude that it is qualitatively the same life force in all of them. We can use the following analogy to demonstrate this: there are many different kinds of electronic devices, all of which have different functions. We have devices that cook food, heat water and wash clothes. We also have devices that provide us with entertainment or even manufacture products. Now, all of these devices may seem like wonderful creations, but without electricity they are all completely useless. Also, although these devices appear to be different, it is the same electrical energy that powers them all and makes them function. This is no different to the energy of life that runs through all living beings. Externally, living beings may appear to be different, and they may even have different bodily functions, but it is the same life force that animates them all.

However, it could be argued that even though it is the same electrical energy that runs through all of our appliances, the electricity still has a beginning, as it is created in a power plant. But, this is not the case, as all a power plant does is convert one type of energy that already exists into another, namely electricity. This takes us back to the fact that energy is never actually created or destroyed, but just transformed and transferred. This, then, may beg the question: if life is energy, and energy can never be destroyed but only transformed and transferred, how do we know that when we die our life force isn't just converted into another form of energy? Well, this is very possible, but the amount of energy can never be destroyed and neither can its fundamental qualities.

Many people believe that the conscious life force cannot exist outside of the body, and can only exist if a body and brain exist. The brain is the organ in the body that processes information gathered by the senses, and is made up of a complex network of neurons and other cells. Many scientists believe that somehow brain activity creates consciousness, and when we sleep, the lack of brain activity reduces consciousness. Some scientists also believe that it may somehow be possible to switch off consciousness in the brain. In a way, it is correct to say that brain activity creates consciousness, and it may even be possible to switch off consciousness, because we previously established that the subjective consciousness principal only becomes aware of itself, or becomes conscious, when the objective world is experienced. However, we also previously established that the consciousness principal is the final observer which eternally exists, regardless of whether or not it experiences an objective world. In fact, although the conscious life force experiences the world through the body, the body's senses and brain are actually limiting what it experiences. This situation is a bit like a person in a house. If a person in a house has all the curtains and blinds open so they can see what is going on outside, not only can they experience the outside world, but the light coming through the windows also enables them to see themselves. This is similar to the life force inside the body looking through the windows of the eyes. If the person in the house then closes all the curtains and blinds so no light whatsoever enters, not only can they no longer see the outside world, but because the room is completely dark, they cannot even see themselves. In this situation, we do not say that the person inside ceases to exist, or even say that the person is reliant on the house and its windows for experience. It is true that whilst the person is confined to the house they are reliant on the windows to see the outside world, and even themselves; however, the person still exists, and as soon as they step outside the house, they can again see both the outside world and themselves. In the same way, just because we close our eyes, ears and other senses so that we are not conscious of the outside world, it does not mean the life force along with its subjective consciousness principal ceases to exist, it just means it is not conscious of the outside world, or even conscious of itself. Similarly, when the body dies, the energy we call the life force still exists, but is simply transferred to another situation where its experience and level of consciousness is restricted by whatever situation it finds itself in. Alternatively, when the body dies, it is possible that the life force may no longer be restricted by any situation or body, but instead attain freedom from physical restrictions, and experience an unlimited, absolute and objective reality.

One subject we haven't yet mentioned is love. Like the concept of good and bad, love is a concept we are all familiar with and a word we often use, but many of us struggle to define what love really is. Because love is something that is central to human life, in order to give a complete explanation on who we are, a thorough explanation of love is required. Strangely, we use the word love not only to describe our relationships with people, but also to describe our relationships with objects, places, situations and even ideas. Therefore, love is a feeling that arises when a person comes into contact with something. However, because we are all different according to our genetic make-up and life conditioning, the people or things that trigger this feeling of love may vary from one person to another. Although we say we have love for certain things, such as love for a type of food, a particular country, a genre of music and so on, we tend to experience the strongest feelings of love for other people. The reason for this is because whilst things such as food, countries and music may possess qualities that provide a great deal of fulfilment, our greatest fulfilment and, therefore, our greatest feeling of happiness, is normally obtained from another life force in the form of another human being. We seem to be instinctively attracted to other living beings, as whenever we make positive connections with them, our own being somehow becomes energised. In fact, when we do not have contact with other people, or even other animals, many of us will experience a deep sense of isolation and loneliness.[6] Anyone who has experienced isolation and loneliness will appreciate how emotionally painful it can be. If a person has no family or friends and lives for many years on their own, although they may eventually get used to the situation, they will probably not experience the same level of fulfilment and happiness as a person who is surrounded by a loving family and good friends. That is not to say that someone living on their own cannot be fulfilled and happy, it is just that most people would find living on their own very difficult.

We have stated that there are different kinds of love; however, most people would consider the true definition of love to be the feeling that arises when one person connects with another. This feeling of love manifests itself in different ways according to the nature of a relationship. For example, paternal and maternal love is where a child gives a great deal of fulfilment to its parents, and because the child is vulnerable, the parents reciprocate by providing protection, nourishment and encouragement. Fraternal and sororal love is where brothers, sisters and friends generally act as equals and form a bond as a result of their common interests and situation. Romantic and erotic love is characterised by a deep sense of attraction; however, romantic love relates more to emotional fulfilment, whereas erotic love relates more to physical fulfilment. There are many

---

[6] Erich Fromm in *The Art of Loving* explains how the basis of our need to love lies in the experience of separateness.

other kinds of relationships that give rise to feelings of love, each having its own characteristics. Sometimes, a variety of loving feelings may even be present at the same time. Regardless of the nature of a relationship, love can be defined as the feeling that arises when one person provides a deep sense of fulfilment to another.

If, as previously stated, all humans are motivated by the desire for life and happiness, and if this feeling of love that we experience when we connect with other living beings gives us one of the strongest feelings of happiness, what does this tell us about who we are? Well, it tells us that life is naturally attracted to life, and this feeling of love that arises when one living being connects with another is one of the greatest feelings, and possibly the most important feeling we can experience. Love, and especially romantic love, can be an overwhelmingly intense feeling. So much so that when we are in a loving relationship, our whole perception of the world changes and the world somehow seems like a much better place. Because this feeling of love is so fulfilling, when a relationship breaks down and love is withdrawn, it can quite literally feel like our whole world has fallen apart. Even the greatest thinkers and rationalists are not immune from feelings of love because love is such a powerful force.

Although we have described love as a feeling, it is not just a feeling, but also an action born out of a feeling. We say that we give and receive love, and this is because when we have this feeling of love it naturally prompts us to be giving of ourselves, and to also open ourselves up to the receiving of others. This constant giving and receiving action creates an ever greater connection between one person and another, which in turn creates an ever greater feeling of closeness and love. When two or more people have this sense of closeness, it creates a relationship whereby they often act as a single unit. A couple in love can sometimes have such a deep sense of unity that they will almost feel like they have become one. Even though each person in the relationship still has their own individual free will, when they are in love, they often act as a unit and act for their common interests. They no longer just act as 'I', but also as 'We'. This reciprocal action of love does not only occur in romantic situations between couples, but in all types of relationships, and even in groups too. Sometimes, a group of friends can feel so close as a result of their common interests that an intense bond can form. This bond also creates a situation whereby the friends act for the common good of the unit. Whether love is a reciprocal action between two people or a group of people, although the individuals may act for the common interests of the unit, this reciprocal action of love ultimately benefits the individuals within it.

Because love is a feeling that becomes intensified through the reciprocal action of giving and receiving, when one person in a relationship withdraws their love, it can have serious emotional effects on the other person, which shouldn't be underestimated or taken lightly. Because we are so attracted to other life, and because love is such an important aspect of our fulfilment, when the object of our love is withdrawn it can leave us feeling incredibly empty. This feeling may take a long time to go away, and in such situations we often try to fill that emptiness with other people or things. It's interesting to see how different people deal with relationship break-ups. We previously stated that the way we view the world is as a result of our genetic make-up and conditioning. If a person's previous life experience has been one of poor relationships, or even abandonment by parents, because they may be conditioned to think negatively about people or have little faith in relationships, they will probably find it difficult to form good relationships. Also, when a relationship breaks down, they may find it difficult to get over. In fact, the greater number of bad relationships a person has, the more a person's negative opinions of people and relationships are reinforced. Similarly, if a person is brought up in a secure, loving family environment and has mainly positive experiences of other people, they are more likely to form good relationships; and, even when a relationship does break down, they will normally find it easier to get over.

Another kind of love that we should explore is self-love. Self-love can be both positive and negative. Self-love is positive when it comes from having a healthy respect for one's self, and where there is a desire to enjoy those aspects of life that promote life and happiness, whilst having equal respect for others. Self-love is negative when it comes from having an unhealthy and unbalanced desire to promote one's self over and above others, whilst having little regard for how others feel. Negative self-love is essentially egotistical, where someone thinks they are the most important person in the world and that the world exists for their pleasure, regardless of what the consequences of their actions may be. The personality that is dominated by negative self-love is a dangerous one. When such demonic, egotistical people attain positions of power, they can have a devastating effect on other people, often suppressing them or even committing genocide. Fortunately, people with extreme egotistical personalities are fairly uncommon; however, because of their desire for self-glory and self-gratification, they often end up in prominent positions of power where they have the greatest opportunity to serve themselves and be served by others. In reality, we are all driven by the desire for self-gratification, but most people instinctively recognise that others have an equal right to fulfilment. That's not to say that the majority of people always act out of a healthy and positive self-love; rather, it's just that most people's personalities are not completely dominated by a negative egotistical self-love, but instead consist of an ever-changing mixture of both.

In respect of our second question 'Who are we?', we can summarise our findings as follows:

**We are a combination of a physical body, mind and conscious life force working together as a single being. Whilst we clearly share much of our biological make-up with other life forms, we also share consciousness and much of our behaviour with other life forms too.**

**The fundamental desire that drives all humans and, arguably, all living beings to act, is the desire for life and happiness. Happiness is a state of consciousness and sense of wellbeing that is experienced when one is fulfilled. Although humans perform all kinds of actions, the desire for life and happiness is the primary motivation that underlies all human activity. Because**

the desire for life and happiness drives all human activity, this shows that life and happiness are the most fundamental requirements of our being.

People have different subjective opinions on whether things are good or bad as a result of individual experience; however, the actual definition of good and bad is a consistent objective principle. Something is good if it promotes life and happiness, and something is bad if it causes destruction and misery. Humans naturally judge things as being either good or bad according to something's perceived ability to promote life and happiness.

All humans arguably act out of selfishness; however, there is a difference between good selfish acts and bad selfish acts. Good selfish acts are those that are born out of knowledge and respect oneself, respect others and promote life and happiness, whereas bad selfish acts are those that are born out of ignorance and do not respect oneself, do not respect others and cause destruction and misery.

Our life force, along with its essential quality of consciousness, is eternal. This is strongly indicated by the fact that everything in the universe is made up of energy, which is neither created nor destroyed, but just transferred and transformed. If everything is made up of eternal energy, our conscious life force must also be eternal energy that possesses the same ability to be transferred, and even possibly transformed.

Love is a feeling that is central to human life. We use the word love to describe fulfilling connections with other people or things. Because humans are attracted to other life forms, we experience the strongest feelings of love for other people. Life is naturally attracted to life, and this feeling of love that arises when one living being connects with another is one of the greatest feelings, and possibly the most important feeling we can experience.

# 3

# WHERE DO WE COME FROM?

We will now attempt to answer the question 'Where do we come from?' Again, we will approach this question from both a scientific and metaphysical point of view. Previously, we stated that the individual self is a combination of a physical body, mind and conscious life force working together as a single being. Therefore, we should explore the origin of the body and mind, as well as the origin of the conscious life force in order to give a comprehensive answer.

Whilst it may be obvious that humans along with other living beings are created through reproduction, it is not so obvious how the human race and other life forms came into being. Currently, the most commonly accepted scientific theory regarding the origin of all life forms is the theory of evolution. Many people are familiar with Charles Darwin and his theory of evolution, but many people are unaware that Darwin did not actually discover the theory of evolution. The concept of evolution existed prior to Darwin; however, Darwin was the first person to explain the process of evolution by natural selection. Although evolution is a widely accepted theory, the evidence to support the theory is still largely missing. Whilst there is clear evidence that evolution happens on a small scale, such as when plants and animals evolve in order to adapt to their local environment,[1] there is, however, little evidence to support evolution occurring on a large scale.[2] The idea that one species evolves into an entirely different species is not supported by the fossil record, and even Darwin recognised this was a problem when he put forward his theory of evolution. Unfortunately, ever since Darwin put forward his theory, this problem has not been adequately resolved. Although recent theories such as punctuated equilibrium[3] (sudden evolutionary bursts) have attempted to explain the lack of evolutionary fossil record, we still have a long way to go in understanding how humans and other life forms came into being. The apparent lack of evolutionary fossil record does not mean that one species did not evolve into an entirely different species, it just means there is inadequate evidence to support the theory. It also means that because the theory of evolution on a large scale lacks strong evidence, promoting the theory as fact is poor science. It is unfortunate that the theory of evolution in

---

1   Microevolution. Darwin's Galapagos Island Finches are a good example of this.

2   Macroevolution. Where major evolutionary changes take place at or above species level.

3   A theory first published in 1972 by Palaeontologists Stephen Jay Gould and Niles Eldredge.

its current form is so commonly presented as almost fact, as scientists and educational institutions are in danger of misleading generations of people in the name of so-called science.

Humans share much of their DNA with other animals, and even with other life forms, and this is one of the main reasons why scientists believe that all life forms gradually evolved from a common ancestor. However, whilst this may or may not be true, it is a poor argument. Just because a computer program is designed by a single person, it does not mean that all computer programs that share similar qualities were developed or gradually evolved directly from their predecessor. Charles Babbage and John Atanasoff may have been the inventors of the first computers, but modern computers are not just products of some gradual evolution of ideas. Many computers and computer programs since Babbage and Atanasoff required radically different thinking in order to produce the kind of computers we use today. On the face of it, this may seem like a poor analogy; however, it is merely demonstrating the point that just because numerous different things share similar core qualities, that does not mean that every single creation as a result of the original idea is a gradual evolution from its predecessor. Completely new ideas may be introduced at any point to meet a certain requirement, thus taking the design in an entirely different direction, whilst at the same time sharing similar qualities to its predecessor. In the same way, although there may be a single origin for all life forms, that doesn't mean they all gradually evolved. It also doesn't mean they didn't gradually evolve. It simply means that whilst we may share much of our DNA with other life forms, this in itself is not adequate proof of large-scale evolution. Despite evolutionary biologists' best attempts at trying to provide concrete evidence to support the theory of evolution, in reality the evidence is, at best, inconclusive. Not only does the fossil record appear not to support the theory of evolution, but scientists also do not fully understand the mechanisms behind it.

The most common non-scientific theories regarding the origin of all life forms are creation and intelligent design. We tend to associate the theory of creation with certain religions, and whilst intelligent design is widely regarded as a distinct theory, many believe it is merely an attempt to rationalise the theory of creation. However, even some scientists believe in intelligent design, as they feel that evolution on its own does not fully explain how such complexity of life came into being. Whilst the theory of intelligent design is not generally considered to be scientific, it could be argued that it is no less scientific than evolution, as neither theories are currently supported by conclusive evidence. One thing we do know for certain, however, is that the universe is extremely old. The belief held by some religious groups that the earth and universe are just a few thousand years old is completely at odds with science. There is now a vast amount of physical, geological and biological evidence proving that the earth and universe are millions, if not billions, of years old. It is hardly surprising that certain religions lack credibility, when they are not prepared to renounce such unfounded beliefs regarding the young age of the universe in the face of overwhelming evidence to the contrary.

That's not to say that the theory of intelligent design doesn't have its merits. In fact, many people justifiably find it difficult to comprehend how such complexity of life and matter exists without there being a conscious intelligent source. If living beings, and particularly humans, possess the ability of intelligent design, why should it not be possible for such an ability to be present in the source of the universe? We previously stated that the sum total of everything that exists has always existed; therefore, the ability of intelligent design displayed by humans must, in fact, exist as a potential within the universe's source. We can logically conclude this because it is not possible for anything in the manifest universe to possess abilities and powers that are greater than its source. It is in one sense academic whether we call the initial formation of the universe the 'Big Bang', or whether we call it 'Creation', as ultimately both are referring to a universe coming into being from a single source. The only thing we really need to establish is, if the universe does arise from a single source, is that source merely inanimate matter and energy, or does it possess life and consciousness? The possibility that the source of the universe may possess life and consciousness is something that has strangely eluded science. Mainly because, historically, science has tried to reduce everything in the universe to gross quantifiable matter, instead of acknowledging that perhaps there are subtle dimensions and realities such as consciousness that can't be reduced or measured by physical means. However, it is relatively easy to establish that if the universe does, in fact, originate from a single source, then that source must possess life and consciousness to at least the same degree as humans do, and probably to an even greater degree. If it didn't, then it would also not be possible for humans and other living beings to possess life and consciousness, as we have already logically concluded that the creation cannot be greater than its source.

If, then, the source of the universe possesses life and consciousness at the highest level, does that mean the universe was created through intelligent design? Well, in a way, yes, but not through the kind of mundane intelligence that humans possess. Although the word 'intelligence' has a broad meaning, we generally define intelligence as the ability to analyse, acquire knowledge, and then apply knowledge in order to solve problems. However, why would an absolute and eternal conscious life force need to acquire knowledge in order to solve problems if it is truly absolute and complete? Also, why would it need to design anything if it is already complete in itself? Well, the answer to both of these questions is, it wouldn't. Whilst the source of the universe must inevitably be the highest and most complete conscious reality, that doesn't necessarily mean it 'intelligently designs' the universe in a mundane human sense. It is just as possible, and very probable, that due to the inherent nature of the universe's source, the universe is actually an inevitable manifestation. We can use the example of light to demonstrate that the universe is an inevitable manifestation of its source. In the same way that white light contains all colours in the colour spectrum, the source of the universe must also contain all realities and possibilities in the universe's spectrum. If, then, all realities and possibilities exist in the universe's source, then the source must be the highest form of life and existence which is only restricted by its boundary with non-existence. Therefore, the universe is merely the full spectrum of dimensions and realities that exists between complete existence and absolute non-existence.

It may be evident that everything in the universe, including life and consciousness, must be present within the universe's source; however, this still doesn't explain how the human race and other life forms came into being. We previously concluded that just because the source of the universe must possess life and consciousness at the highest level, that does not automatically mean that the universe was created through some kind of mundane intelligent design. The truth is that the theory of intelligent design does have its merits, because consciousness is something we know exists. However, the theory of evolution also has its merits, as we know that life forms evolve on a small scale in order to adapt to their local environment. It is, in fact, very possible that a number of theories are true to some degree, and the universe, along with all life forms contained within it, came into existence through a combination of creation by intelligent design and evolution.

Although evolution, creation and intelligent design are the most common theories explaining the origin of all life forms, there are other less mainstream theories too. However, until we come up with conclusive evidence to support any theory on how humans and other life forms came into existence, for now we have to be satisfied with being able to say that whilst all life forms do have an ultimate source, we simply don't fully understand the mechanisms that created them. Also, regardless of what name we choose to give that ultimate source, it must contain within it the full spectrum of realities, dimensions and powers that are manifest in the universe, including life and consciousness.

We will now briefly try to establish how the mind arises; however, before doing so, we will first define what the mind is. Unfortunately, there doesn't appear to be a commonly accepted precise definition of the mind, as the mind means different things to different people. Therefore, we will use the most general definition and define the mind as the faculty of thought, memory and reason. Although the mind appears to be reliant on the brain for its formation, it is more important to note that the mind is really a mode of consciousness. Previously, we stated that consciousness is the subjective principal observer that becomes aware when it experiences the objective world. We also previously stated that whilst the life force and consciousness principal is confined to the body, it is reliant on the body for experience. Therefore, the mind is an imprint left on the consciousness as a result of the brain's neural activity. However, this imprint is constantly changing as the conscious life force interacts with the world through the body's senses. When the senses are stimulated by objects, this information is fed back to the brain where neural activity creates an impression on the consciousness, much in the same way as a photographic image makes an impression on paper. Because the conscious life force is driven by the desire for life and happiness, when it experiences pleasure and pain, these impressions are recorded on the consciousness via the brain. Through accumulated experience, the conscious life force is also then able to make decisions via the brain. Therefore, we can conclude that the mind is simply an imprint on the consciousness that arises when the conscious life force interacts with the objective world via the body. Of course, many neuroscientists wouldn't accept this definition, as they either do not make a distinction between mind and consciousness, or do not believe that the mind and experience rests on anything.[4]

Now that we have briefly looked at how the mind arises, we should next consider what the source of our individual conscious life force is. We previously established that because everything in the universe consists of energy, our conscious life force must also consist of energy. We also previously stated that energy eternally exists, and whilst it may appear to have a beginning and an end, it is, in fact, just transferred and transformed. Therefore, we should naturally conclude that our conscious life force must have existed prior to being born, either in its current state, or in a different state of energy. Even if we don't try to understand what

---

[4] This is a notoriously difficult subject, and one that cannot be adequately explored in a book of this length. However, when drawing a conclusion, it should be remembered that not even the body can create something from nothing – not consciousness, or even what consciousness is made of. It must arise from something pre-existing, but is not necessarily contingent.

the meaning of life is, it simply doesn't seem reasonable that one day we were born from nowhere, then after a period of time, we cease to exist again, for no apparent reason. This just doesn't sit comfortably with many people. It doesn't sit comfortably because not only is it the fundamental nature of all living beings to want life, but the idea that life has a beginning and an end actually goes against the laws of science, particularly the law of conservation of energy. Many people would argue that a person only believes in a before and afterlife because they cannot come to terms with death. However, whilst this may be true, it is also completely natural that we fear death, as it is not the nature of anything in the universe to have a true beginning or end. As previously stated, the sum total of everything in existence has always existed, and will always exist in one form or another; therefore, it is not surprising that the idea of absolute non-existence should be so difficult for a person to accept.

If, then, we accept that our conscious life force existed prior to being born, where did it come from? Well, this is fairly straightforward to establish. If the universe's source contains the full spectrum of possible existence, including life and consciousness, then our conscious life force must have also originated from that same source. However, just because our conscious life force originated from the universe's source, that does not necessarily mean it came directly from its source into the body. Although the Big Bang, or Creation, may have been the initial act that set the universe in motion, a great deal has happened since then. In the same way, although our conscious life force originated from the universe's source, it is possible that it has existed in other forms or realities since it came forth from its source. This may seem extremely unlikely to some, but is it really any more unlikely than the theory of evolution? Why should it not be possible for our conscious life force to evolve through different bodily forms, if we know that energy can be transferred from one thing to another? This concept of the transmigration of the soul from one body to another is more commonly known as reincarnation.[5] The doctrine of reincarnation tends to be associated with the religions of Hinduism and Buddhism, although it has actually been a widespread belief for thousands of years. Many ancient cultures, including a number of ancient Greek philosophers, believed in some form of reincarnation. There have even been Jewish, Christian and Muslim sects that believed in reincarnation, although these religions generally consider the doctrine to be a heresy.[6] Of course, just because reincarnation has been a widespread belief for thousands of years, that doesn't necessarily mean it is a credible theory. However, because scientifically reincarnation is not out of the question, and because many cultures, and even some of our most influential philosophers such as Pythagoras, Socrates and Plato believed in some form of reincarnation, we should give it serious consideration.

---

[5] For a beautiful and profound description on the nature of the soul/self, and how it transmigrates through different bodily forms, see The Bhagavad-Gita (Chap. 2, 12-30).

[6] The Cathars believed in reincarnation. Some followers of the Kabbalah and even some Sufis believe in reincarnation.

Reincarnation is a very interesting concept, although due to Western culture being so heavily influenced by the monotheistic religions of Judaism and Christianity, until fairly recently it has not been a widely accepted doctrine in the West. However, reincarnation has gained huge popularity in recent years, mainly because many people feel that the concept more adequately deals with certain questions that the large monotheistic religions have struggled to give convincing answers to. Arguably, the greatest of these questions is 'If there is a god, why is there so much suffering in the world?' This is a valid question; however, it is only a valid question if God is seen as some anthropomorphic being that is directly responsible for both creating and governing the universe. It is not a valid question though, if God is merely seen as the impartial source of the universe and has no business with its creation or maintenance, other than being the source of the powers inherent within it. Where God is just the impartial source, there is a much greater emphasis on the individual conscious life force, or soul, being responsible for its own destiny, and this is where reincarnation comes in. The doctrine of reincarnation is normally accompanied by the doctrine of karma or action. Combined, they form the belief that the life we live now is as a result of actions performed in a previous life, and the actions performed during this life will directly influence what happens to our conscious life force upon the body's death. Reincarnation is not just limited to the so-called rewards or punishments that we may receive as a result of good or bad deeds, but also encompasses the belief that whatever actions we perform will have a direct impact on the way our mind and consciousness develops. In fact, every action we perform has an impact on the way our mind is shaped, although we don't normally notice this as the process is very gradual. However, by repeatedly engaging in the same kind of activities, our mind and consciousness are subtly moulded to habitually think and feel in a certain way. Therefore, reincarnation is also the belief that upon the body's death, the soul will acquire another body or situation that reflects the evolving nature of the mind and consciousness. We understand that even in this life, the actions we perform have both a direct and indirect effect on the way our mind and consciousness develop. We also understand that the actions we perform will lead us to situations in life where we will experience either happiness or misery. Therefore, although reincarnation cannot currently be proved or disproved, it does have a kind of logic to it, as it seems to reflect the fact that we all possess free will, our actions will have certain outcomes and we are all ultimately responsible for our own actions.

Not only do the mainstream monotheistic religions seem unable to give a satisfactory explanation as to why there is so much suffering in the world, but they also seem unable to explain why all humans are not born equal. If there is a god that is directly responsible for creating and governing everything in the universe, and if it is believed that we only live once, then why are so many people born into misery with little hope of escape? This is not just a question of why some people are born into poverty, but also a question of why some people are born into situations that are not conducive to developing a positive and healthy outlook on life. For example, some people are born into families where they are subjected to extreme abuse from an early age. There is now a significant body of evidence to suggest that if a person suffers abuse or neglect as a child, they are less likely to form positive relationships or become successful later on in life, and much more likely to go on to commit criminal acts. In other words, if God is directly responsible for creating and governing everything in the universe, then it would appear that God is also responsible for putting people into situations where they are more likely to commit so-called 'sinful acts'. Many religious people would argue that, whilst we don't always understand why God puts people into certain situations, it is always for their own good. This, however, doesn't seem like a satisfactory answer. A more acceptable answer would be: because the source of the universe (whether you call it God or any other name) possesses all possible realities present in the manifest universe, it is already complete in itself and has no requirement to create or govern the universe. Therefore, the universe and all beings within it are inevitable manifestations that represent the full spectrum of all possible realities between complete existence and absolute non-existence. In addition to this, we can say that whilst our individual conscious life force also has its origin in the universe's source, because we are not all born equal, and because we all possess free will, it is very possible that our individual conscious life force existed in another body or situation immediately prior to entering its current body. Therefore, although we may not know what situation we were in prior to this life, we should at least acknowledge that we are all responsible for our own actions, and reflect on the possibility that we may have performed actions in a previous existence that directly influenced the kind of life we have now. That's not to say that a person is born into a certain situation in life only as a result of previous good or bad actions, there may be other factors at play too, such as choice.[7] We often see that although some people are born into situations that appear to be conducive to a happy life, such as possessing wealth, good looks, fame and so on, it is not always the case that such individuals go on to be happy. In fact, without certain character traits some wealthy and famous people end up becoming emotionally tortured individuals as a result of what their situation brings them. In the same way, although some people are born into situations that do not appear to be conducive to a happy life, such as being born into poverty or having a disability, it is not always the case that such individuals are unhappy. Although our past actions may have directly influenced the kind of life we have now, we should be very careful in judging what we consider to be a good life. Sometimes what appears to be a good situation can actually end up being a curse, and what appears to be a bad situation can end up being a blessing.

It could still be argued that if the source of the universe is impartial, why do we possess free will? Well, as we have previously stated, because the

---

[7] For an entertaining account on how choice may play a role in reincarnation, see 'The Myth of Er' in Plato's *Republic*.

universe cannot be greater than its source, free will in an unrestricted and absolute form must also be present within the universe's source. Of course, some people believe that we do not actually possess free will, and that our choices are determined by a number of variables, such as our genetic make-up, environment and conditioning. However, even if our choices are completely determined, that doesn't mean we do not possess free will, as free will is simply the ability to make choices, regardless of whether those choices are determined or not.[8] The ego also plays a significant role in the choices we make, where we place ourselves at the centre of the universe as the principal enjoyer. Although the ego clearly exists, because it is essentially a negative expression of the self, it does not seem reasonable that such a negative quality exists within the universe's source. In fact, it is likely that the ego is the divisive quality that actually separates the self from its source. Our egocentric conscious life force cannot recognise its full potential whilst it is detached from the universe's source, because by definition the egocentric individual foolishly thinks they are self-sufficient. However, the idea of self-sufficiency is a complete delusion, as we have already established that the subjective consciousness principal is reliant on an objective reality in order for it to possess consciousness. Even from a material point of view no one is truly self-sufficient, because from the day we are born until the day we die, we all rely on other people and the environment for our existence.

---

[8] This is the view of Compatibilism.

In respect of our third question 'Where do we come from?', we can summarise our findings as follows:

**Although it is obvious that humans along with other living beings are created through reproduction, it is not so obvious how the human race and other life forms came into being. Currently, the most common theories regarding how we came into being are evolution, creation and intelligent design. Whilst the theories of intelligent design and evolution both have their merits, neither of them are currently supported by conclusive evidence. It is, however, very possible that a number of theories are true to some degree, and the universe along with all life forms contained within it came into existence through a combination of creation by intelligent design and evolution.**

**In respect of the mind, although it appears to be reliant on the brain for its formation, it is more important to note that the mind is really a mode of consciousness. In the same way as a photographic image makes an impression on paper, the mind is merely an impression left on the consciousness as a result of the brain's neural activity.**

**Because energy eternally exists, our conscious life force must have existed prior to being born, either in its current state, or in a different state of energy. Also, if we can logically conclude that the universe's source contains the full spectrum of all possible existence, including life and consciousness, then our conscious**

life force must have also originated from that same source.

Because energy can be transferred from one thing to another, it is very possible that our conscious life force is also transferred from one body or situation to another through a process of transmigration.

Just because our conscious life force originated from the universe's source, that does not necessarily mean it came directly from its source into the body. Although we may not know what situation our conscious life force was in immediately prior to the current body, if the source of the universe is complete and impartial, and if we possess free will, it would appear that we are all ultimately responsible for the kind of body or situation we find ourselves in now.

# 4

# WHAT IS THE GOAL OF LIFE?

So what is the goal of life? Well, this is a relatively easy question to answer. Previously, a comprehensive explanation was given on how the desire for life and happiness is the desire that underpins everything we and all living beings do. Therefore, the goal of life is to attain complete life and happiness. We actually already possess eternal life, but a lack of true knowledge regarding the fundamental nature of life and the universe means that many people are unaware that their conscious life force is eternal. A lack of true knowledge, and the absence of positive actions that spring from true knowledge, results in people living in fear of pain and death. This fear of pain and death is one of the main contributory factors why we don't experience complete happiness. Life and happiness go hand in hand as you cannot experience happiness without possessing life. Therefore, if we accept that our conscious life force is already eternal, then the true goal of life is simply to attain complete happiness.

Although we may acknowledge our conscious life force as being eternal, that doesn't mean we already possess 'complete' life, as our level of consciousness is incomplete. We previously stated that although our conscious life force is eternal, it relies on an objective reality for it to be aware of itself. Whilst in the body the conscious life force experiences different aspects of the universe through the body's senses. However, not only do the senses limit what the conscious life force experiences but also, the physical universe can only provide it with a limited amount of happiness. The reason for this lies in the fact that although the universe represents a spectrum of powers and realities present within the universe's source, because we are unable to experience every aspect of existence simultaneously, we cannot experience the totality and completeness of life. At any given moment our conscious life force can only experience a limited number of dimensions and realities present within the universe's spectrum. Therefore, it would be natural to conclude that if we want to experience complete life and happiness, then this can only be achieved by experiencing the source of the universe itself, where the full spectrum of dimensions, powers and realities exist in completeness. We can once again use the example of light to demonstrate this. When we look at the colour spectrum, we are merely observing the different colours present within white light; however, if we want to experience all of these colours simultaneously, then this can only be achieved by looking at white light. It is no accident that when you see illustrations of the Big Bang theory, the single point that the universe emanates from is often depicted as a brilliant white light. It is also no accident that many religions portray the highest possible reality, whether it be called God, Brahman, Nirvana, Enlightenment or any other name, as a brilliant white light. This is because science and certain religions have come to the conclusion that the source of the universe must contain the full spectrum of powers manifest in the universe in a single complete reality, even if some scientists misleadingly call that complete reality 'nothing'.

When we refer to the word 'knowledge' we are ultimately referring to consciousness, as without consciousness, there can be no knowledge. We may possess knowledge of many things in life, but that knowledge will always be incomplete so long as our consciousness remains restricted by our limited senses. Therefore, complete knowledge is actually complete consciousness, which is only attainable by reconnecting with the universe's source. The more we acquire true knowledge, the happier we become. The first step in acquiring true knowledge is to understand that the sum total of everything that exists, including life and consciousness, will always exist… it is eternal. Attaining this first step in knowledge will give us great peace; then, once we have understood the eternal nature of life, we can go on to contemplate who we are, where we come from, what the goal of life is and how we should live. Ignorance is truly the root of all misery in life. When we fail to understand what is beneficial for us, when we disrespect ourselves and others, when we engage in destructive behaviour, we do so out of ignorance because we lack the knowledge that such things will ultimately bring about our downfall. When we live in ignorance, we also lack the strength and power to overcome obstacles and shape our own destiny. Knowledge, however, is the root of all happiness, because when we possess true knowledge, we possess greater consciousness and greater fulfillment in life. Knowledge is also the strength that gives us the ability to have greater control over our destiny, both here and in the hereafter.

Although we can conclude that the goal of life is complete happiness, which can only be obtained by experiencing or reconnecting with the universe's source, it should also be remembered that we have free will. As individual living beings we choose the way we live our lives; however, we shouldn't forget that the choices we make in life end up defining what we are and how we experience the world around us. The goal of life is not to own a nice home, to have lots of money, to possess power and so on; rather, the goal of life is happiness. We only desire material things as we believe they will bring us happiness. However, whilst material objects can provide us with a degree of happiness, because they are limited dimensional realities, they cannot give us complete happiness as they do not possess everything that our conscious life force requires to be completely fulfilled. Even those things in life that give us a great deal of happiness are temporary, and we often spend much of our time working hard trying to maintain them. And, even those individuals that are wealthy enough to be able to maintain a luxurious life style, can at any time be struck down by serious illness, be victims of war or suffer from some other calamity. So many rich and famous people who, on the surface, appear to have everything in life, end up being victims of law suits, suffer from depression or even commit suicide. The reality is that regardless of our situation in life, our existence in this world is always precarious. Until we truly understand how fragile our lives really are, and until we understand what the root cause of our misery is, we will not seek true knowledge that leads to the complete happiness our conscious life force so desires.

Our conscious life force can only be fulfilled if it has something missing and possesses a certain capacity to be fulfilled. Therefore, our conscious life force in its complete state is full of life, full of an objective reality. That objective reality is the source of the universe, which consists of absolute and complete existence. Therefore, if the source of the universe gives fulfilment to our conscious life force, it must also be responsible for its enlightenment. So, how can we describe what the source of the universe is like? For thousands of years, humans have tried to define the universe's source and have given it different qualities. Humans have also created many religions and cults to facilitate the worship of the universe's source in the hope of attaining eternal life and happiness. It has also been given many different names such as God, Brahman, Nirvana and so on. However, it is not the name we give to the universe's source that is important, but the concept and understanding of what lies behind that name. For example, the word 'God' may mean different things to different people, and over the years the word 'God' has taken on quite negative connotations. Whilst many religious books describe God as possessing positive qualities such as love and compassion, the same books also describe God as possessing very negative qualities such as wrath and anger.[1] However, if the universe's source is complete and absolute, how can it possibly experience wrath and anger? Wrath and anger are emotions that we experience when we are frustrated and unhappy, and we only experience these emotions when we are not fulfilled. Therefore, if God experiences negative emotions such as wrath and anger, then God cannot be complete and absolute. In reality, however, the source of the universe is complete and absolute, and because it possesses the full spectrum of powers manifest in the universe in a single complete reality, it lacks nothing and does not experience negative emotions.

Scientists and atheists often criticise those who believe in God. However, it is not always the actual belief in God or a superior life force that is really being criticised, but people's immature ideas on the nature of God. So many people who believe in God see God as some limited anthropomorphic being. They try to project mundane human qualities onto God. A good example of this is where God is seen as the father. In one sense, God may be like a father because the universe's source is the origin of all life… it is the seed-giving father, but this concept is often taken too literally, whereby God is also depicted as an old man residing in the heavens. In fact, if it is believed that God has a bodily form, then this is to believe that the source of the universe possesses

---

[1] For example, in the Christian Bible (NIV), Deuteronomy 6:15 says 'for the LORD your God, who is among you, is a jealous God and his anger will burn against you, and he will destroy you from the face of the land.' But then, in 1 John 4:16, it says 'God is love. Whoever lives in love lives in God, and God in them.'

attributes that are adapted to and limited by a specific material environment. But, how can the source of the universe possibly be limited by the very environment it supposedly created? Trying to define the universe's source by using mundane qualities is actually a reflection of human ignorance.

There are many belief systems in the world, and at different times in history some have been more prominent than others. The following are brief descriptions of the most common belief systems, both religious and non-religious.

**AGNOSTICISM**

Agnosticism is the belief that certain truths, especially those pertaining to the existence of God, are unknown or cannot be known. It is derived from the Greek *agnosis* (without knowledge). There are two main kinds of agnosticism, hard and soft. Hard agnosticism (also known as strict, strong, or closed agnosticism) is the belief that it is not possible to know whether God exists or not, whereas soft agnosticism (also known as empirical, weak or open agnosticism) is simply the position that a person does not know whether God exists or not.

**ATHEISM**

Atheism is the belief that God or gods do not exist. It is the opposite of theism and is derived from the Greek *atheos* (without God). Although atheism rejects the belief in a personal god, it also often rejects the belief in any form of higher spiritual reality, or even life after death.

## THEISM

Theism is the belief that at least one god exists. It is the opposite of atheism and is derived from the Greek *theos* (God). It is more specifically the belief in a personal god or deity, a god that creates and governs the universe. Theism does not reject the existence of many gods, it is merely the belief that God or gods exist.

## MONOTHEISM

Monotheism is the belief that there is only one god. It is also the belief that God is the sole creator and governor of the universe. It is derived from the Greek *monos theos* (single god). Four of the world's largest religions are generally considered to be exclusively monotheistic – Judaism, Christianity, Islam and Sikhism, and whilst these religions vary greatly in their doctrines and practices, they share the common belief that there is only one true God that should be worshipped.

## HENOTHEISM

Henotheism is the belief in and worship of a single god, whilst accepting that other gods exist or may exist.

It is derived from the Greek *henas theos* (one god). Henotheism shares elements of both monotheism and polytheism, whereby a single god is worshipped over and above other gods. Certain branches of Hinduism are henotheistic, although the ancient religions of Rome, Greece and Egypt are further examples of religions that became henotheistic.

**POLYTHEISM**

Polytheism is the belief in and worship of many gods. It is derived from the Greek *poly theos* (many gods). Some branches of Hinduism, as well as many ancient and tribal religions, are considered to be polytheistic. In polytheism, a pantheon of gods with varying degrees of importance are worshipped for specific purposes. However, when one god is singled out and worshipped over and above all other gods, then polytheism becomes henotheism.

**PANTHEISM**

Pantheism is the belief that the universe is identical with God, or all is God. It is derived from the Greek *pan theos* (all God). Pantheism rejects the idea that God is distinct and separate from the universe. The pantheistic view is that God can be experienced in the world around us, and those who consider themselves as pantheists often have a deep reverence for nature. Pantheism as a concept or belief system is ancient, and is present to a greater or lesser degree in many of the world's oldest religions, philosophies and cultures.

## PANENTHEISM

Panentheism is the belief that everything is in God. It is derived from the Greek *pan en theos* (all in God). It is the belief that God is an unlimited and eternal spiritual reality that is distinct from the universe, whilst at the same time permeating everything within it. God is essentially seen as the soul of the universe. In panentheism, the universe is a manifestation of God, and although God pervades everything in the universe, God still transcends it. Panentheism should not be confused with pantheism. In pantheism, God is seen as being identical to the universe, whereas in panentheism, God is seen as being distinct from the universe. Panentheism is a fairly common belief system and is present in many of the world's religions and philosophies, both ancient and modern.

## DUALISM

Dualism is the theory of two distinct and separate entities or realities. It is derived from the Latin *duo* (two). In philosophy, it is the belief that there are two distinct substances, mind and matter. In theology, it is the belief that the world is ruled by two opposite forces, good and evil.

## MONISM

Monism is the belief that there is only one substance or reality. It is derived from the Greek *monos* (single). The monistic view is that although many different things exist, they are all merely manifestations or modes of a single reality.

With the possible exception of agnosticism, the world's philosophies and religions incorporate one or more of the above belief systems. It could be argued that even atheism has its place in some religions, such as Buddhism, Jainism and traditional Chinese religions, although these religions are only atheistic in the narrowest definition of the word as they don't believe in a personal god. However, because over the years the commonly accepted definition of atheism has widened to also include the rejection of all higher spiritual realities, in the modern sense of the word, these religions aren't really atheistic as they all believe in a higher spiritual dimension.

Although it may not be possible to empirically prove whether a superior life force exists or not, this should not stop us pondering the goal of life. Even scientists do not rely on empirical evidence alone to formulate theories, but often use a number of different approaches and techniques to ensure their theories are consistent. As already outlined, it is possible to give very robust arguments demonstrating the eternal nature of existence, and it is not such a great leap in our understanding to appreciate that everything in life has a basis. However, trying to understand the nature of the universe purely through the science of physics, without trying to understand the fundamental nature of life and consciousness, is a one-dimensional and flawed approach. The best theories are those that are consistent when considered from many different viewpoints.

Although scientists and atheists often question the motives of those who believe in God or a superior life force, one also has to question the motives of those who believe in agnosticism or atheism. The main problem with hard agnosticism is that the individual who states they are a hard agnostic, does so on the understanding that the human brain and senses are limited. However, if a person understands that their brain and senses are limited, how can they then go on to say that it is categorically not possible to know whether God exists or not if their understanding is imperfect? In other words, they have contradicted themselves. In fact, if a person accepts that their brain and senses are limited, and as a result does not know whether God exists, it is much safer for that person to simply say that THEY do not know whether God exists or not. To take it a step further and say it is not possible to know whether God exists is essentially justifying a lack of understanding.

Similarly, what is it that motivates someone to become an atheist? Is it because there are valid arguments that can disprove the existence of a superior life force? Or is it because atheists simply reject many of the superstitions and irrational doctrines that religions often believe in? It is true that some myths, superstitions and beliefs held by certain religions are very difficult to accept; however, whilst this may be a reason to reject a particular religion, it isn't a reason to not believe in a superior life force. Whilst atheists are sometimes considered to be intelligent in the general sense of the word, they are often misinformed about philosophy and religion, and the arguments put forward by atheists are often very weak.

Atheists base their beliefs on a number of arguments, the main ones being: 1) Because of the presence of evil in the world, an all-powerful and perfect God cannot exist; 2) There is lack of empirical evidence proving God's existence; 3) The theory of evolution by natural selection explains how all living beings came into existence; therefore, the belief in God is no longer valid. In respect of the atheist's argument regarding the presence of evil in the world, we have previously stated that this argument is only valid if God is directly responsible for creating and governing the universe. However, if God is merely the impartial source of the universe and has no direct business with its creation or maintenance, and if the universe and all beings within it are simply inevitable manifestations representing the full spectrum of all possible realities between complete existence and absolute non-existence, then the presence of evil does not hold up as a valid argument disproving God's existence. In respect of the argument stating that there is a lack of empirical evidence proving God's existence, a lack of empirical evidence is simply that, and does not prove or disprove anything. It is generally accepted that prior to the 15th century, Europeans were unaware that North America, South America or even Australia existed. However, just because there appeared to be no evidence to support their existence, that doesn't mean they didn't exist. In fact, many people would argue that the existence of life and consciousness are very good indicators that God or a superior life force does exist. As for the argument stating that the theory of evolution by natural selection means that God does not exist, this is a very poor argument. As previously mentioned, the theory of evolution on a large scale is a theory that is yet to be proven. However, even if it is possible to empirically prove the theory of evolution by natural selection, that doesn't mean that God or a superior life force doesn't exist; rather, it just means that the creation theories presented by certain religions, especially by the Judeo-Christian tradition, are incorrect. Unfortunately, atheists who believe that the theory of evolution is an alternative to God, seem to be missing the fundamental point that the universe still requires an original cause, and that cause must itself be uncaused[2] and contain everything manifest in the universe, including life and consciousness. To deny the universe's source, the qualities of life and consciousness is unscientific, as these are things that exist in the manifest universe. The other problem with atheism is that whilst it tries to present arguments to disprove the existence of God, it has not come up with a credible alternative theory explaining the fundamental nature of life, the nature and origin of consciousness, the basis of the human need for love and happiness, the basis of morality and the eternal nature of existence. There is also a need to clarify what atheism is. Although atheism rejects the

---

[2] Also see Aristotle's 'Unmoved Mover', *Physics*, Book 8, and *Metaphysics*, Book 12.

existence of God, it is sometimes the case that an atheist is actually rejecting the existence of a personal God, and may still believe in an impersonal superior life force or some universal consciousness.

Other than pantheism, most of the world's belief systems are fairly well defined, even if there is a degree of overlap. In the case of pantheism, although it is considered to be an ancient belief system, in ancient times the reverence for nature would have been inevitable as people would have been much more exposed to the powers of nature. However, the greatest issue with pantheism as a belief system is that it is essentially no different to atheism, as it rejects the idea of a distinct and separate god or superior life force. In fact, because God is not actually defined, it could be argued that pantheism is no different to general materialism and is not really a distinct belief system at all.

There is a belief, especially within Hindu philosophy and spirituality, that the world's religions are simply many paths up the same mountain. Whilst this analogy has its limitations, it is a convenient way of describing the world's religions. If the mountain's summit is seen as the highest possible spiritual reality, then the different religions are simply different paths to the summit. However, whilst a person is on their particular religious path, because the mountain is so large they are often unaware that there are other routes to the top. Sometimes the different paths meet, and upon coming across other paths, the religious person may come to any one of the following four conclusions.

1. Although I have not yet reached the top of the mountain, based on my experience of the journey so far, not only do these other paths appear to not lead to the summit, but they also don't meet the descriptions in my guide books (religious texts). Therefore, I will remain on my current path as it is quite clearly the correct and only path to the summit.

2. Whilst these other paths appear to go to the top of the mountain, they are of poor quality and do not appear to be direct routes. My guide books state that there are other, lesser paths on this mountain and to be wary of them. Therefore, I will remain on my current path as it is quite clearly the best one to reach the summit.

3. I am aware there are many different guide books describing the various paths to the top of the mountain; however, although these other paths may lead to the top, my current path is the one that leads directly from my home town. This is the path everyone in my home town recommends, and it was the path our ancestors took. Therefore, out of convenience and a fear of the unknown, I shall remain on my current path as it must surely take me to the summit.

4. I had no idea there may be other paths leading to the top of the mountain, although other than the guide books that describe my currant path, I have not read any other guide books describing other

paths. Therefore, I will keep an open mind and try an alternative route for a short way, and if it appears to be a less treacherous and more direct path to the summit than the one I am currently on, then I will continue on that alternative path.

Conclusion 1 is the conclusion of the dogmatic religious person who cannot possibly imagine there is any religious path other than their own. Conclusion 2 is the conclusion of the religious person who is a little more open-minded, but whilst recognising similarities between their own religion and others, still believes their religious path to be the best. Conclusion 3 is the conclusion of a reasonably open-minded religious person, but due to cultural conditioning, opts to follow the religious path of the culture they were born into, as it is the easiest and most familiar. Conclusion 4 is the conclusion of a truly open-minded person who is not concerned with cultural conditioning or held back by fear. Although this person may make errors of judgement, they try to learn from their mistakes and see past the relative cultural conditioning of religion. This person's objective is to reach the summit of truth that is supposed to be at the heart of all religions, and not to simply follow a guide book.[3]

Although it is true that some paths may not lead to the summit at all, or that a particular path may be the quickest route to the top of the spiritual mountain, that does not mean there is only one path to the top. Also,

---

[3] Ramakrishna, the 19th century Indian mystic, is a noteworthy example of such a person.

whilst a person is on a particular path, the summit appears different depending on their particular viewpoint. From one side of the mountain the summit may look like a sharp peak, but from the other side it may look like a series of craggy rocks. This is a similar situation to the different religious views on the nature of the absolute truth. From the relative perspective of one religion the summit may seem like a personal god, but from the perspective of another it may appear to be like an unlimited and formless spiritual reality. However, the closer a person gets to the summit, the better their understanding becomes. It is only when a person has reached the top of the mountain that not only do they have a clear understanding of what the summit is like, but they also realise that there are, in fact, many other paths that converge at the top.

It is interesting to see that at a popular level, religions can appear to be very different to each other. However, when you look at the more mystical, esoteric or monastic aspects of many religions, there is often little difference. The Christian monk, the Buddhist monk, the Sufi, the Hassidic Jew and the Hindu mystic sometimes have much more in common with each other spiritually, than they do with the less devout followers of their own religion. Maybe this is because they are all a little closer to the summit of the spiritual mountain, and have a much clearer view than some other members of their own religion who are still floundering at its base.

Whilst practicing a particular religion may be helpful to some, if a person simply follows the external trappings of a religion without understanding the nature of life and consciousness, then religion may actually be a hindrance to spiritual development. Religions are merely frameworks designed to help people attain a higher objective; however, if a person loses sight of that higher objective and only follows the external practices, then religion is empty. Unfortunately, so many religions teach us to develop noble qualities such as love and compassion, but instead of carefully adhering to such teachings, their followers are busy arguing and fighting over minor differences in doctrine. It's hardly surprising many people cannot take religion seriously when there is so much hypocrisy within it.

Another problem with many religions is the inconsistency of the teachings found within their scriptures. Although many religious texts contain profound spiritual insights, they also often contain what appear to be contradictory statements and dubious moral teachings. Therefore, all religions should be understood within the context of the cultures they were born out of. Also, because we have no way of knowing how accurately the life and teachings of their founders and prophets were documented, translated and interpreted, we should never blindly accept the teachings of any religion.

Regardless of a person's religion or lack of religion, we are all responsible for our own actions. If we want true advancement in life, then our first step is to recognise that spiritually, we are all related and we all share the same desire to be happy. We may not currently understand what will make us truly happy, but if we can put love, compassion and respect at the heart of everything we do, then slowly we will understand. Being a member of a religion does not make a person good, just as not being a member of a religion does not make a person bad. As we have previously concluded, the definition of good is anything that promotes life and happiness; therefore, the truly good person is the person that tries to promote life and happiness in everything they do. It is the good person that attains peace and happiness, because it is the good person that is ultimately fulfilling the nature of their being.

If most religions have a similar goal, why are they so often enemies? If the common goal of many religions is to worship or attain a higher spiritual reality, then why do they not show greater respect for each other? Unfortunately, many religious people are too quick to judge other religions by their external cultural traditions, rather than first trying to understand their core beliefs, which are often similar to their own. Most people who follow a particular religion sincerely believe it to be the best religion. However, it often never crosses the religious person's mind that there are billions of other people in the world who follow a different religion, but also sincerely believe their religion to be the best one. Although sometimes there are clear differences in doctrine between one religion and another, there are often many similarities. In the same way that science and religion should remain open-minded and try to work together in a spirit of mutual respect, it is time that the world's religions also work together in a spirit of mutual respect. That's not to say that the different religions and science will, or should, always agree, but even where there are differences in opinion there should be respect. Of course, in reality this isn't always possible, as quite often religious groups and scientific organisations do not have the greater good of humanity at the heart of what they do; however, where there is common ground they should always attempt to build bridges.

Regardless of whether a person follows a particular religion or not, there are certain fundamental truths that lie at the heart of everything we experience and do. It was previously established that the eternal nature of existence, the fundamental desire for life and happiness, and defining things as being either good or bad on the basis of their perceived ability to promote life and happiness, are all consistent principles that transcend subjective opinion. It was also previously established that the universe's source must contain the full spectrum of dimensions, powers and realities manifest in the universe, including life and consciousness, as the universe cannot contain anything greater than its source. We therefore concluded that if we want to experience complete life, then this can only be achieved by experiencing the source of the universe itself. If, then, a person recognises that only the universe's source can provide complete fulfilment to their conscious life force, wouldn't it be natural to want to experience or reconnect with the universe's source? Well, yes, and this is arguably the goal of most religions, even if their understanding is sometimes lacking, their methods questionable and their followers often insincere. One may then ask 'What is the nature of the universe's source?' However, this is not such an easy question to answer. We may use all kinds of analogies and metaphors, but really we should not expect to understand the nature of the universe's source through our limited senses. As already mentioned, names such as God, Brahman, Nirvana, Supreme Being, Universal Soul and so on, can only hint at a higher reality. We may also use different concepts to try and understand the universe's source, but by doing so we are in danger of projecting limited mundane qualities on to an absolute reality that ultimately cannot be defined.[4] Trying to define the universe's source with our limited senses, is like trying to define white light when we have only ever experienced the colour spectrum that makes up white light. However, if we truly come to understand that existence is eternal, and that complete life and happiness is our ultimate goal, then all around us we will find powerful clues as to what the nature of the universe's source is like. Of course, many people will reject such words as being religious nonsense. However, understanding the true nature of life and consciousness, and understanding our place in the universe, ultimately has little to do with religion and everything to do with acquiring true knowledge and taking responsibility for our own actions in life.

To attain complete life and happiness means following a process of reconnecting with the universe's source. However, this process is not defined by performing certain rituals or refraining from certain activities; rather, it is defined by our inner attitude to life. If we adopt an attitude of love in everything we do, then we will naturally avoid negative destructive

---

4   Some schools of Hinduism, especially Advaita Vedanta, believe that Brahman (God) cannot be defined using limited physical qualities and, therefore, choose to describe it as 'neti neti' ('not this, not this'). The 12th century Jewish philosopher Maimonides had a similar approach.

behaviour, and instead, act in a way that promotes life and happiness, both in ourselves and in others. Also, we should not misunderstand the universe's source as being limited by space and time. We should not think of it as either being outside ourselves or inside ourselves, as it transcends such definitions. Instead, the reconnecting with the universe's source is a spiritual process that leads to the awakening of our being. Although this process is a spiritual one, success isn't reliant on being a member of a particular religion or organisation. If a religion or organisation doesn't promote life and happiness in everything it does, and if it doesn't teach the reconnecting with the universe's source through a process of love, compassion and respect, then we should reject it. Treading this spiritual path is fraught with difficulties, and because we are impelled to act in a certain way as a result of our genetic make-up and conditioning, we will inevitably make many mistakes. But, even if we repeatedly make mistakes, this shouldn't dissuade us from following this process of self-realisation. We should endeavour to train our minds to think good thoughts, as from good thoughts, good actions will naturally follow. Every good thought or deed that promotes life and happiness is a small step towards reconnecting with the universe's source and, therefore, is a step towards gaining greater life and happiness. It is said 'Our life is shaped by our mind; we become what we think. Joy follows a pure thought like a shadow that never leaves.'[5] Of course, as we possess free will, we can

---

5   The Dhammapada 1:2, translation by Eknath Easwaran.

either make the decision to serve our egocentric self and remain disconnected from the universe's source, or we can walk the path of self-realisation and try to attain complete life and happiness. The choice is ours.

In respect of our fourth question 'What is the goal of life?', we can summarise our findings as follows:

**The goal of life is to attain complete life and happiness. Although we already possess eternal life, a lack of true knowledge regarding the fundamental nature of life and the universe means that many people are unaware that their conscious life force is already eternal. However, if we accept that our conscious life force is eternal, then the true goal of life is simply to attain complete happiness.**

**Although our conscious life force is eternal, because our body's senses are limited, and because we are unable to experience every aspect of existence simultaneously, we cannot experience the totality and completeness of life. Therefore, it would be natural to conclude that if we want to experience complete life and happiness, then this can only be achieved by experiencing the source of the universe itself, where the full spectrum of dimensions, powers and realities exist in completeness.**

**The goal of life is not to possess wealth or power, but to possess happiness. We only desire material things as we believe they will bring us happiness. However, whilst material things can provide us with a degree of happiness, because they are limited dimensional**

realities, they cannot give us complete happiness as they do not possess everything that our conscious life force requires to be completely fulfilled.

Our conscious life force can only be fulfilled if it has something missing, and possesses a certain capacity to be fulfilled. Therefore, our conscious life force in its complete state is full of life, full of an objective reality. That objective reality is the source of the universe and consists of absolute and complete existence.

There are many different belief systems in the world, both religious and non-religious. Whilst scientists and atheists often question the motives of those who believe in God or a superior life force, one also has to question the motives of those who believe in agnosticism or atheism. The problem with hard agnosticism is that it is essentially a contradiction, whereas atheism is often based on very weak arguments and is yet to come up with a credible alternative theory explaining certain fundamental aspects of life.

Religions are simply frameworks designed to help people attain a higher objective. If a person loses sight of that higher objective and only follows the external processes, then religion is empty. Therefore, in order to attain complete life and happiness, one has to follow a process of reconnecting with the universe's source. However, this process is not defined by performing certain rituals or refraining from certain activities, but instead is defined by an inner attitude of love.

As we possess free will, we can either make the decision to serve our egocentric self and remain disconnected from the universe's source, or we can walk the path of self-realisation and try to attain complete life and happiness. The choice is ours.

# 5

# HOW SHOULD WE LIVE?

In order to answer the question 'How should we live?', we must first answer the question 'How should we measure success and advancement?' This may seem a reasonable question, and one that is often asked at a personal, national and even global level; however, the answer isn't necessarily obvious. Many, if not most, people would agree that it is important to measure success and advancement, and we often try to do so by measuring our wealth, status, power and so on. However, are things such as wealth, status and power reliable ways of measuring success and advancement? Well, clearly no. Wealth may be a measure of how successful someone is in business, but not all wealthy people are wholly responsible for creating their own wealth. Sometimes, wealth along with status and power are inherited, gifted or won; therefore, in circumstances where little or no effort has been made in obtaining wealth, status or power, it is not reasonable to say that such things are a good way of measuring success. In order to have success you need to succeed in something, and in order to succeed, effort is required. If, then, a person obtains wealth, status or power through their own efforts, can we safely conclude that they are successful? Well, again no, as some of the wealthiest and most influential individuals are also some of the unhappiest. Most people will know of a wealthy, famous or powerful person who has had a drug or alcohol problem, has suffered from depression, or has even committed suicide. Can we truly say that people are successful on the basis of their wealth, status or power? Absolutely not.

Similarly, technology cannot be considered a true measure of advancement. Although humans have been exploiting their environment and developing new ways of living for thousands of years, up until the industrial revolution technological advancements were fairly basic by today's standards, and many of the world's ecosystems were still largely intact. However, since the industrial revolution humans have been inventing, developing and manufacturing on such a large scale that it has led to the wholesale destruction of our environment, which is possibly threatening the long-term viability of human existence. How can the mass destruction of our environment, which has resulted in the most basic requirements of life such as clean air and water not being freely available to many, be considered advancement? How can the invention and proliferation of weapons of mass destruction be considered advancement?

Previously, we concluded that the ultimate goal of life is to attain complete life and happiness. Therefore, if this is our goal then we should measure success and advancement by this criterion, and not by personal wealth, status, power, economic growth, technological advancement, or any other criteria. As we already possess life, albeit incompletely, personal success should simply be measured by our level and consistency of happiness. If we want to measure success on a national or global scale, then the level and consistency of happiness should be measured across the entire population; and, if it is found that large sectors of society are predominantly unhappy, then we would need to question the kind of society that allows for such disparity. Success and advancement are closely related, and if we want to measure advancement, then this should also be measured by how happy or fulfilled we are. If our happiness is increasing, then this should be considered an advancement; if our happiness is decreasing, then this should be considered a regression. It should also be noted that the happier we become, the more complete our life becomes.

Some people will argue that if we can increase the human lifespan then this would also be an advancement; however, we should be careful in considering this as a true advancement. The reason being is that not only is our conscious life force already eternal, but even under the best conditions the human body is genetically predisposed to only live a certain length of time. Of course, it is good to live a healthy lifestyle and we should consider it a success if we can maximise our lifespan by doing so, but without artificial means, the human body will only naturally last for a certain period. Although many people would consider the ability to extend the human lifespan by artificial means an advancement, such an idea is rooted in ignorance and a fundamental lack of understanding as to the eternal nature of life and consciousness. That doesn't mean we can attain complete life and happiness by just getting rid of the body. The body is simply a reflection of the conditioned conscious life force, and in order to attain complete life and happiness, it requires an inner change, a change away from serving the egocentric self, to one where we put the promotion of life and happiness through a process of love at the heart of everything we do.

Of course, in reality humans are not making the most of their situation, and success and advancement are not currently measured by people's level of happiness. Instead, we find huge inequality in the world which is fueling instability. Essentially, human ignorance has resulted in the precarious global situation we now find ourselves in. Some people will point to religion as being the cause of the world's problems, but this just isn't the case, as not all religion is bad. Other people will point to political ideology as being the cause of the world's problems; however, whilst certain political ideologies have led to destruction and suffering on a huge scale, they are not responsible for all of the world's problems. Some may even point the finger at science; yet, whilst science has certainly been grossly negligent in the way it has allowed certain information to become available for inappropriate use, it is not ultimately responsible for all of the world's problems. It is also often said that money is the root of all evil, but again, this isn't the case, as money is just an inanimate object. Instead, it is human ignorance that lies at the heart of all of the world's man-made problems. It is the presence of ignorance within religion that makes certain aspects of religion abhorrent, not the concept of religion itself, which is nothing more than a widely recognised system of beliefs and practices. It is the presence of ignorance within politics that makes certain political ideologies threatening, not the concept of politics itself, which is just the theory and practice of governing people. And, ironically, it is the presence of ignorance within science that makes its misuse dangerous, not the concept of science itself, which is simply the systematic pursuit and application of knowledge. As for money, it is ridiculous to say that it is the root of all evil, as money is just an instrument that represents the value of something. In fact, it is greed born of ignorance that makes money appear to be the cause of so many problems, not money itself.

Although humans are responsible for many of the world's problems, they are not responsible for all of them. There are many things in life that we have little control over, such as being struck down by certain illnesses, being affected by natural disasters or even the way other people may act; however, it is the way we respond to such things that is important. Ironically, even though many scientists and atheists reject the belief in an eternal conscious life force, they are still busy trying to manipulate the body and environment in order to improve and extend life. In other words, they still ultimately value the principle of life. But, rather than taking the time to analyse the fundamental nature of life and consciousness, scientists try to improve and extend life by manipulating the body and environment with their imperfect knowledge, often with dire consequences. It is not technological advancement that will save mankind, but spiritual development. It may not be possible to have complete control over what happens to us and our environment, but if we want to live in a happier and more peaceful society, then this can only really be achieved by recognising that spiritually we are all related, and by treating each other with love, compassion and respect.

The world is a complex place, and even if we put noble qualities such as love, compassion and respect at the heart of everything we do, it is still often difficult to know the best course of action, as we don't always understand the consequences of our actions. For example, we may provide aid to a poor country, but instead of that aid helping the people it was intended for, it may get into the hands of rebel groups who use it to promote their own dangerous political agendas, causing further misery. Or, we may provide education to people who do not have access to it, but instead of empowering people to create better lives for themselves, education may sometimes empower individuals to create misery and destruction. Doing the right thing can often be difficult, but this should not stop us from trying. We should give careful consideration to the way we live and the impact it has on ourselves, others and the environment. The more we understand any situation in life, the better placed we are to make an informed decision on the best course of action. Also, we have become so conditioned by modern life that we now consider the reliance on technology to be the norm. We have largely lost touch with a natural way of life, and whilst in some respects this may be good, in other respects it is not, as it has resulted in humans being seriously out of balance with the environment they depend on. Not only is the destruction of our environment threatening our future existence, but it is likely that aspects of our modern lifestyle are responsible for the increase in certain illnesses, health conditions and diseases. If the human race is to stand any chance of surviving, then it needs to take a very large step back, look at the greater picture, and have a monumental shift in its attitude. Unfortunately, we cannot rely on world leaders or anybody else to do this for us; therefore, we all have to take responsibility for our own actions. We may not be able to change the world, but we can change ourselves, and if we recognise that we are something other than just a physical body, and if we want to attain lasting happiness, then it is down to us to act. Becoming a better person will not only benefit ourselves, but it will benefit others too, as our positive actions will also promote life and happiness in the wider world. It may seem like a heavy burden to always be mindful of our actions, but it can be done. Although we will inevitably make many mistakes, and although it requires huge determination, the spiritual path is a simple process that will increasingly fill us with happiness.

The spiritual path is not about following rituals or being a member of a religion, although this may be helpful to some; it is about changing our attitude and approach to life in general. Unfortunately, modern culture seems to have become completely dominated by consumerism; however, the world's rapidly growing consumer population is creating an ever-increasing demand on the world's resources, a situation which is unsustainable.[1] Whenever we purchase and consume anything, consideration should be given to the impact it has on ourselves, other living beings and the environment. Although nature can be cruel, and one of its fundamental principles is that one being lives off another, if we have a genuine respect for life, then we should always aim to minimise the negative impact our actions may have. Wherever possible, we should only take from the world what is required for our wellbeing and happiness. With the mass production of goods on a global scale, it can be very difficult to know what effect the products we consume are having on ourselves and others. However, if we endeavour as much as is realistically possible to practise a thoughtful and caring approach, we can significantly improve our situation. In respect of our own wellbeing, the things we consume should give personal fulfilment and build physical and mental health. Our experiences should promote life and happiness and not create negative, destructive behaviour. In respect of other living beings, the things we consume should respect their right to life and should not cause unnecessary suffering. Although it is important to respect other people, we should also make animal welfare a top priority. Finally, we should give careful thought to how our actions impact the environment, as all living beings depend on it. When consuming anything, we should consider how an item's

---

[1] For an informative guide on the global effects of consumerism, see Worldwatch Institute's State of the World 2010: Transforming Cultures from Consumerism to Sustainability.

production, distribution, method of sale and disposal effects the environment. Special care should be taken with regards to our use of non-biodegradable materials such as plastics, as not only are they having a devastating effect on our planet now, but they will continue to do so for generations to come.

From a spiritual point of view, it may seem unnecessary to give an explanation on how we should live; however, although we are spiritual beings, most, if not all, people are still acting on the level of the egocentric self as expressed through the body. Whilst our conscious life force is limited and bound by the body, it is important that we respect it and maintain it in good health. Just because we come to an intellectual understanding that our conscious life force is eternal, until we transform ourselves spiritually and attain greater life and happiness, it is vital that we take a practical approach to the mind and body's requirements. There are certain key aspects to everyone's life, and we shall now take a brief look at these and explore how we can benefit both ourselves and others by having a considerate approach.

**DIET**

If we want to understand what the natural human diet is, then we need to look at the characteristics of the human body, what Palaeolithic man ate and what our closest extant relatives eat. Firstly, humans are clearly omnivores as we are generalised feeders; our digestive system is intermediate between carnivore and herbivore as it can process both plant and animal foods, and we possess canine teeth. Although humans do not need to eat meat, and although other great apes also possess canine teeth but eat little or no animal protein, they still have the ability to do so. Secondly, we have a good idea what Palaeolithic man ate, and this, again, clearly suggests that humans are omnivores. Throughout the Palaeolithic period, humans ate a mixture of vegetables, fruits, nuts, seeds, flowers, mushrooms, meat, fish, insects, eggs and honey. Contrary to popular belief, recent findings suggest that Palaeolithic man may have only consumed modest quantities of meat; however, the type of environment and the availability of other food sources would have largely determined how reliant Palaeolithic man was on animal protein. Although some grains and legumes were also consumed, it is generally thought that large quantities of these were not consumed until the advent of agriculture at the beginning of the Neolithic period, around 12,000 years ago. It is also believed that dairy products were not consumed at all until the Neolithic period, and neither were refined sugars. Another important feature of Palaeolithic man's diet is that unlike today, most meat would have been low in fat as the diet of consumed animals would have been different and the animals would have also been more active, resulting in leaner meat. Finally, we will compare our diet with our closest extant hominid relatives – chimpanzees, gorillas and orangutans. Although it is well-documented that chimpanzees eat small amounts of meat, their diet is largely plant-based. Also, although it is generally believed that gorillas and orangutans only eat plants and sometimes insects, they have the ability to eat meat and recent observations suggest they may very occasionally do so.[2]

Therefore, from the above we can safely assume that although humans are omnivores, it is probably not natural for us to eat large quantities of meat. We can also say that large quantities of fatty meats, refined grains, legumes, dairy products and refined sugars are not part of our natural diet. With regards to salt, although it is essential for the body's survival, and although it has been used as a preservative for thousands of years, we should avoid consuming too much of it.

Just because our natural diet may not include significant quantities of certain foods, that doesn't necessarily mean they are bad for us, as the human body is capable of adapting to a wide variety of foods. However, the modern Western diet, which consists of large quantities of saturated fats, carbohydrates and salt, is clearly not good for us, and has resulted in a sharp increase in diet-related diseases and conditions such as cardiovascular disease, diabetes and obesity. Of course, exercise is also an important factor, but many people are simply unaware of the fact that an impractical amount of exercise would be required to burn off the large number of calories many people are now consuming. Unfortunately, much of the

---

[2] Wild Sumatran orangutans have been observed eating slow lorises. Also, an inconclusive study by The Max Planck Institute for Evolutionary Anthropology, published by *National Geographic* (7 March 2010), found DNA from monkeys and forest antelopes in the faeces of wild African mountain gorillas.

information about diet and exercise is provided by the media, food companies and health product companies, who often have a financial interest in what they are promoting and is, therefore, not always reliable.

Certain foodstuffs are clearly unnatural for humans to consume, and these include dairy products. Although many people would be surprised to hear this, the evidence is quite clear. Not only are humans the only mammals to consume milk into adulthood, but they are also the only mammals to consume the milk of other mammals. Although some mammals such as cats and dogs will consume the milk of other mammals if given to them, this would not happen in the wild and the milk often makes them ill. Milk has the very specific function of providing balanced nutrition to young mammals until they are able to digest and obtain other types of food. Most mammals are weaned at an early age, and this normally corresponds with a natural decrease in the enzyme lactase. Lactase is essential for breaking down the sugar lactose in milk, and if lactase is not present then mammals struggle to digest milk properly. This is the reason why most of the world's human population is lactose intolerant to a greater or lesser degree, and why it is clearly unnatural for humans and other mammals to drink milk or consume dairy products into adulthood. Although certain dairy products are easier for humans to digest, it still doesn't change the fact that humans shouldn't be consuming the milk of other mammals. Also, milk has widely been promoted as a vital source of calcium that helps prevent certain conditions such as osteoporosis; however, research suggests that this may not be the case. Strangely, countries that consume some of the largest quantities of dairy products also have some of the highest rates of osteoporosis, whilst countries that consume some of the lowest amounts have some of the lowest rates of osteoporosis. Of course, further research needs to be done as there may be other contributory factors. Although research is inconclusive, some scientific studies also strongly suggest that consuming dairy products may have just as many adverse health effects as beneficial ones; therefore, it is highly questionable whether we should be consuming them at all, especially when there are many other foods that are a good source of calcium.

In order to understand what we should be eating, we must also understand what purpose food serves. This may seem obvious, but humans, and especially Westernised societies, seem to have lost their way when it comes to diet. Firstly, we must understand that the main purpose of food is to provide balanced nutrition to the body. Although some foods that are high in fat, sugar or salt may be considered unhealthy, most people understand that we require such things in our diet, and if we eat these foods in moderation, then they are actually beneficial to our health. Secondly, food is a source of great pleasure, and if it didn't taste and smell good, then we would be less inclined to eat it. Finally, we tend to be attracted to food that is visually appealing, so great care is taken in the way food is presented in order to encourage us to eat it. All of the above are important considerations when producing, purchasing and consuming food. However, Westernised societies are now placing far too much emphasis on how food tastes and the way it is presented, and not enough emphasis on its nutritional value, which after all, is the most important thing. We can, therefore, conclude that, whilst it is important for food to taste good and be visually appealing, because the primary function of food is to provide balanced nutrition to the body, we should judge how good food is mainly on its ability to provide the right nutrition. We can also conclude that, based on our understanding of the human body, and based on the diet of Palaeolithic man and other extant hominids, the natural human diet should mainly consist of vegetables, fruits, nuts, seeds, legumes, flowers, mushrooms, fish, insects, eggs and honey. Although we can also eat refined grains and sugars, we should try to limit our intake of these. As omnivores, we also have the option to eat meat. However, we should probably avoid eating large quantities of fatty or red meat as there is growing evidence that eating too much of either is not good for us, although this may be down to modern farming methods or the way it is processed as much as anything else.

Whilst it is fairly well-documented that eating a Palaeolithic type diet has many health benefits, it should be noted that modern humans are quite different from our hunter-gatherer ancestors, and we may no longer be as well-adapted to a Palaeolithic diet as we once were. However, the small number of studies that have been undertaken show that in addition to weight loss, eating a Palaeolithic diet may also help reduce blood pressure and cholesterol.[3]

---

[3] See Frassetto et al. 'Metabolic and physiologic improvements from consuming a paleolithic, hunter-gatherer type diet'. *European Journal of Clinical Nutrition* (11 February 2009).

Although the purpose of eating a balanced nutritious diet is to promote health and happiness, we should also give careful consideration to how the food we produce and consume effects the environment and other living beings. Animals are often reared in atrocious conditions and experience untold suffering just so we can gratify our tongues and bellies. We should question how civilised we really are if we support such suffering, and if we cannot obtain ethically produced meat, fish or eggs,[4] then we should drastically reduce or even eliminate these food sources from our diet.

**HEALTH**

Good health is essential for living a happy and fulfilling life. If we suffer from poor health, not only do we find it difficult to function properly, but our desire for life also becomes diminished. Of course, diet is key to enjoying good health, but there are numerous other aspects of life that play an important role in both our physical and mental wellbeing. Our physical and mental health are connected, and people have known for a long time that one directly influences the other; therefore, it is important to understand that the choices we make have an impact on the quality of our life as a whole. For example, we now know that the food we eat affects our mood, and our mood affects the body's immune system. However, although this is relatively common knowledge,

---

4   It is questionable whether eating meat, fish or eggs can ever be ethical.

and although most people understand the importance of good health, it is surprising to see that so many people still make poor lifestyle choices.

Whilst poor health is often linked to poverty, the connection is misleading as there are a number of socio-economic factors that influence health. People from poor nations often have relatively healthy diets and may also experience low levels of mental illness. However, because they also have poor hygiene, poor sanitation and few medical facilities, average life expectancy is normally low. In many developed nations the opposite is actually true. Although people from wealthy nations often have unhealthy diets and suffer from high levels of mental illness, because they benefit from good hygiene, good sanitation and good health care, average life expectancy is normally high. What this goes to show is that life expectancy does not always reflect the state of a nation's health. In fact, the high average life expectancy enjoyed by many wealthy nations is largely a result of medical and technological advancements, and not due to people living healthier lifestyles. However, medicine and technology are not true advancements, but inadequate solutions that are masking the reality of people's unhealthy lifestyle choices. That's not to say that medicine and technology have no place in the world, but if we want to live healthier lives then we have got to tackle the root of the problem.

Not only are things such as poor diet, excessive alcohol consumption, smoking and a lack of exercise responsible for poor health, but there is increasing evidence that environmental pollution, along with the chemicals found in everyday products, are also responsible for a sharp increase in certain illnesses such as cancer. Unfortunately, most people now live such complex and unnatural lives that it is often difficult to establish the root cause of many medical conditions. Modern humans have moved so far away from what is considered to be a natural lifestyle, it is hardly surprising our health is suffering as a result. Although it is difficult to avoid many of the negative consequences of living a modern lifestyle, it is possible to significantly reduce them. However, when it comes to health, nobody but ourselves can improve the situation. Even if we are fortunate enough to have access to good healthcare, we are all ultimately responsible for our own wellbeing. Therefore, if we want to enjoy good health, it is essential that we make the effort to understand what constitutes a healthy lifestyle and adjust our lives accordingly.

**REST**

Along with our other basic requirements, adequate rest is crucial for maintaining a healthy mind and body. When we talk about rest, we are referring to rest and relaxation whilst awake, as well as sleep, both of which are important. There is now a significant body of evidence that suggests that not getting enough quality sleep can have serious health implications. Sleep is a regenerative process the body goes through in order for it to continue to function properly. Although having the occasional poor night's sleep will not significantly impact our quality of life, if we regularly do not get enough sleep, then not only can it lead to illness, but we may also suffer from fatigue, concentration problems, stress and moodiness. Studies also suggest that there may be a link between having too much sleep and certain medical problems such as diabetes, obesity and heart disease; however, it is not currently clear how much poor lifestyle is also a contributory factor. Having too much sleep is also often a sign that there are aspects of our waking life that need addressing, such as depression, although depression may be the cause or consequence of either too little or too much sleep. It should also be noted that lifestyle directly affects our quality of sleep, and our attitude to life and the activities we undertake are critical to the body's ability to rest and regenerate itself. As sleep is a regenerative process that takes up a significant part of our lives, we should not underestimate how important it is. It is now generally accepted that adults require 7 to 9 hours sleep a night; however, this amount increases significantly for babies and children.[5] Although the amount of sleep required will vary from one person to another, it is essential that we understand our own sleep requirements, and that all forms of rest are kept in balance with other aspects of our lives in order to maintain a healthy mind and body.

---

[5] National Sleep Foundation's sleep time duration recommendations: methodology and results summary, *Sleep Health* (March 2015, Vol. 1, Issue 1, pp. 40-43).

**RELATIONSHIPS**

Nobody is an island, and it is natural for us to want to engage with other people in fulfilling relationships. However, far too often we put our own interests above the interests of others, often resulting in conflict. Although it is important to have our own best interests at heart, it shouldn't be at the expense of others. Positive relationships start from an understanding that deep down we are all essentially the same. We may look different, have different personalities and hold different beliefs, nevertheless we are all spiritual beings that possess the same fundamental desire for life and happiness, even if that desire is expressed in a variety of ways. There are many different kinds of relationships, but in order for any of them to be successful they must be based on love and respect. Of course, sometimes we find ourselves in negative and destructive relationships through little fault of our own, and in these situations it is important for us to understand the best course of action. Although we should always show compassion towards others, if the other person in a relationship is not prepared to renounce negative qualities such as hate, anger and aggression, there comes a point where, for our own peace of mind, we have to quietly walk away. Some relationships are destined to fail from the outset because they are built on poor foundations. A good example of this is where people become friends as a result of sharing an unhealthy interest in something destructive or brutal. Instead of that friendship promoting unity and happiness, it will probably reinforce each other's negative thoughts and behaviour, with potentially disastrous consequences. Another example is where a romantic relationship is entered into out of a deep sense of insecurity. Although we are all a little insecure at times, if a person with low self-esteem enters into a relationship, it will often manifest itself as jealousy or an over-dependency on the partner to provide emotional support. Romantic relationships where one or both partners are very insecure, will inevitably be difficult; therefore, before entering into any serious relationship it is important that we have sufficient self-respect.

We all have emotional and physical needs, and within reason our natural urges should be satisfied. Understanding our emotional and sexual urges can be confusing as they are a complex mix of our genetic make-up and experiences. From a spiritual perspective, sexual relationships are often seen as selfish gratification; however, whilst there may be truth in this, for most people it is not healthy to supress sexual urges too much, as suppression often manifests itself through other undesirable behaviour. There should be a balance of satisfying our natural urges in a positive way that helps promote good relationships. Sexual acts and fantasies that incorporate dark thoughts, force, violence, pain and a lack of respect for others are mentally and emotionally destructive, and should be avoided at all costs.

Relationships often break down due to a lack of communication. Whilst it can be good to express how we feel to others, it is just as important to listen and understand how others feel. Sometimes, we are hurt by the way a friend, family member or partner acts and it can be difficult to forgive them; however, our emotional pain can often completely cloud our judgement, resulting in rash decisions. In such situations, we should take a step back and try to understand the circumstances that led to the hurtful actions. If we look at the situation objectively, we may be surprised to learn that under the same circumstances, we may have acted in the same hurtful way. Although forgiveness is important for successful relationships, there will always be situations where we feel that forgiveness is not possible. Where there seems to be no hope of reconciliation, sometimes it is better to accept the situation and move on. Relationships can be complicated, and when they break down, there is rarely an easy solution. However, if we can develop genuine self-respect, and if we can show love and compassion even to those who cause us pain, then not only will we have greater inner peace, but we will also build positive and meaningful relationships.

**CONFLICT**

Conflict is an unfortunate part of life and occurs at a personal, local, national and global level. Ultimately, conflict is a result of the egocentric self clashing with other egocentric selves in the struggle for existence and, with the exception of personal inner conflict, is the root cause of many of the world's man-made problems. Naturally, we all have our own interests at heart, but when we put our own interests above those of others, then conflict occurs. Of course, in reality conflict is often more complicated than this, and it can be difficult to disentangle its origins, yet all conflicts can be reduced to this basic principle. Many of the world's worst conflicts have occurred because their perpetrators believed that their culture, religion or political ideology was somehow superior to that of others. Believing this, numerous misguided conquerors and dictators have committed heinous crimes, whereby not only have they suppressed other nations, but they have also tortured and killed their own people. History shows us that when cultural, religious or political ideologies are forced upon others, it often results in devastation and misery. Unfortunately, this ignorant and egotistical mentality still persists in the world, and will no doubt continue to do so. Even if a person believes that their culture or views are superior, nobody has the right to forcibly impose them on others. We always have a right to defend ourselves, but never a right to be an aggressor. Everybody should have the freedom to live their life the way they choose, providing it does not unreasonably encroach on the lives of others. Even if someone chooses a life of gross ignorance, that is their choice, and it is not our business to force our own views and lifestyle on them, providing they are not harming anybody else. If we hold views that we genuinely believe to be superior to those of others, then those views should be offered and promoted by peaceful means, and never by force.

Sometimes, conflict occurs at the most basic level of survival. For example, a person, region or country may not have access to an adequate water supply, or access to enough land to produce food. In these circumstances, we should carefully consider how fairly land and resources have been divided among the world's population… we will, no doubt, come to the conclusion that huge inequality exists. Of course, because global equality is extremely unlikely, the world's population is growing, and land and resources are finite, we should expect conflict to be a standard feature of this world. This may seem a depressing thought to many, but it is an unfortunate reality. The nature of this world is that every living being that occupies it is driven by an egocentric self. The result of this is that one being lives at the expense of another, rather than living in harmony. Some people believe that because religious and political ideologies appear to be responsible for many of the world's conflicts, if we dispose of these things, then the world would somehow be a wonderful place. However, this belief is based on a false notion. Even if all religious and political ideologies were disposed of, egocentric human beings would still exist and conflict would still occur. The idea of a world utopia is a complete delusion, as it is inconsistent with the reality of human nature and the natural world. Although we cannot escape this reality, if we acquire true knowledge, make the effort to change ourselves, and live a life based on love, compassion and respect, not only will we largely transcend the miseries of this world, but we will also avoid creating unnecessary conflict and suffering. In this world there will always be differences of opinion and a struggle for survival, and it is inevitable that on occasions, we will come in to conflict with others. But, providing we can justify our existence by living an ethical life, then we will always have the right to defend ourselves.

**ENVIRONMENT**

When we think of the environment, we tend to think about the wider environment of fields, forests, mountains, rivers, oceans and so on. Many people are now aware of the importance of respecting the environment, yet it continues to be destroyed at an alarming rate. This is partly due to human greed, and partly due to a profound lack of understanding that we are all dependent on a healthy environment for our physical and mental wellbeing. Although environmental issues are currently at the forefront of people's minds, not enough is being done to stem the tide of destruction. The issue is not just one of population, but also one of individual consumption. As more countries become developed, increasing numbers of people are becoming mass consumers, putting huge pressure on the world's ecosystems. Unfortunately, unless drastic action is taken at a personal, national and global level, the world will become an increasingly polluted and unpleasant place to live, which will inevitably give rise to conflict as people compete for resources.

Not only do we rely on the environment for things such as clean air, water and food, but we also rely on it for our mental wellbeing. Most people appreciate the beauty of nature and derive great joy from simple pleasures, such as walking through a forest or swimming in the sea. However, we are rapidly creating a world where these natural pleasures are becoming increasingly difficult to enjoy. Imagine a world where it is no longer possible to stroll along an unspoilt beach because of overdevelopment and pollution. Imagine a world where we can no longer experience a sunlit forest because the forests have been cut down or killed by acid rain. Imagine a world where it is no longer possible to enjoy a beautiful panoramic view because the landscape is completely littered with buildings, open cast mines, pylons, wind turbines, solar panels and agricultural plastic. Actually, it is not so hard to imagine, as we are all witnessing this gradual degradation of our environment. Is this the kind of world we want to live in? Are we prepared to sacrifice the beauty of our planet in order that we can feed our egos, enjoy consumer products and create a world of convenience? Anyone who believes that the creation of such a world is advancement, is not only blind to their own inner beauty, but also blind to how important beauty is to their own mental and spiritual wellbeing.

The burning of fossil fuels is currently one of the main contributory factors leading to the destruction of our planet; however, instead of tackling the root cause of the problem by significantly reducing our energy consumption, we instead create 'clean energies' in the vain hope that we can go on consuming the planet in a less harmful way. Although renewable energies can play an important role in reducing carbon emissions, we are fooling ourselves if we believe that renewable energies such as wind, solar and hydro power are the solution to our environmental problems. In order to meet the energy demands of a rapidly increasing consumer population, not only would vast amounts of the world's resources be needed to build the infrastructure required for creating so-called clean energy, but our environment would also be completely blighted in the process. If the world's resources were properly and fairly managed, our planet would no doubt be able to support a vast population. However, the time is rapidly approaching where if humans are to survive and have any quality of life, then not only have we got to create and implement practical and humane solutions for managing the size of the world's population, but we also need to significantly reduce our consumption of the world's resources. In reality, we can only achieve this if we have a shift in perception and live simpler lives.

Humans are not only destroying the world through the consumption of vast quantities of energy, raw materials and manufactured goods, but they are also destroying it through the negligent disposal of waste. Although waste created by manufacturing processes can sometimes be recycled or turned into useful by-products, the reality is that dangerous wastes such as chemicals, heavy metals and pesticides are being released into the environment on a phenomenal scale. Although this problem is often more acute in developing nations due to the absence of adequate measures to control pollution, it is also a huge problem in developed nations due to the greater consumption of raw materials and manufactured goods.

Another serious threat to the environment is the use of non-biodegradable materials such as plastics. A wide variety of consumer goods and packaging materials are now made from plastic. However, although plastic recycling has been introduced in many countries, far too much plastic is being put into landfills or is being left to litter the environment. The most striking example of this is the shocking amount of plastic that is now floating around in our oceans.[6] This plastic is not only killing birds and marine life, but it is also breaking down into tiny particles and entering the food chain, a truly worrying thought. Of course, we shouldn't ignore how cruel nature can be, and it is only natural for humans to want to create better lives for themselves and not be at the mercy of nature; however, if the human race is to stand any chance of surviving, then we must get our priorities right and start respecting the environment.

The word 'environment' may also refer to the immediate environment of our home, or the local environment of the place where we live, both of which are important aspects of life that should be briefly considered. Our home is important as we spend so much time in it, but people often place too much or too little importance in having a nice home. Not only does owning more than one home, or owning a home that is too large or ostentatious, have a much greater impact on the environment than a modest one, but it may also be a reflection of a person's egocentric mentality. Similarly, a home that is poorly maintained, dirty or full of clutter may be a reflection of a person's general lack of care. Just

---

6   See *Science*, 'Plastic waste inputs from land into the ocean' (12 February 2015, Vol. 347, Issue 6223, pp. 768-771).

as the immediate environment we create for ourselves can be a reflection of our state of mind, our immediate environment can also have a direct impact on our wellbeing. Whilst we should not place too much emphasis on having a nice home, according to our means we should ensure that it is a positive, bright, clean, comfortable and simple environment that promotes physical and mental wellbeing. Similarly, the place, village, town or city where we live should also be a positive environment. Living in a place that is dirty and run down, or a place that suffers from high rates of crime and violence, is obviously not conducive to living a happy life, and where possible such places should be avoided. We can, therefore, conclude that although it may not be possible to have complete control over our environment, we should always try to minimise the negative impact our actions have on the wider environment, and according to our means, live in a home and place that promotes physical and mental wellbeing.

**EDUCATION**

It is widely accepted that education empowers people to create better lives for themselves. It is therefore surprising to see how so many countries currently lack good education systems, or have education systems that fail to teach children the most basic life skills required to create happy lives for themselves. Inadequate education systems are not only found in developing nations, but in developed ones too, although wealthy nations have little excuse when it comes to failing people through poor education. Not only are children not being taught the important subjects of diet, hygiene, health, financial management and ethics, but there is also an overemphasis on teaching certain technical subjects such as mathematics and science, much of which is forgotten later on in life. In some countries, there is also the problem of educational institutions applying too much pressure on children to succeed, often resulting in children suffering from low self-esteem when they fail. Finally, the widespread practice of teaching religious dogma in schools is creating narrow-minded people everywhere, something that is surely not conducive to creating a more peaceful world.

Children's minds are incredibly malleable, and have the ability to acquire large amounts of information in a short period of time. Therefore, it is crucial that children are given a well-balanced education as it forms the foundation of who they become and what they achieve later on in life. It is unfortunate that so much emphasis is placed on teaching children certain subjects at the expense of other important ones. What is the point in teaching children subjects at an advanced level if, as adults, their lives are ruined by obesity and crippling debt because they have not been taught the basics of diet and financial management? And what is the point in encouraging children to pursue a higher education if they have not even been taught how to respect themselves and others? If children are to develop into well-rounded and happy human beings, then basic life skills must be taught from an early age.

Although children often have no control over the quality of their education, or little control over the subjects they are taught in school, as adults we do have control over such matters. Whilst not everyone has the opportunity to go into higher education, this shouldn't dissuade us from improving ourselves when we become adults. However, if we want to develop into successful and happy adults, then we must seize whatever opportunities are available to us, and this includes acquiring basic life skills. It doesn't matter how intelligent a person is, if they cannot maintain their body and mind in good health, if they cannot manage their finances, and if they don't know how to respect themselves and others, then their so-called 'intelligence' is of little use. Regardless of our circumstances in life, it is crucial for us all to learn the basic life skills of diet, hygiene, health, financial management and ethics, as it is these skills that will form the basis of a happy life.

**WORK**

Work can be defined as those activities that are undertaken to obtain what is required to maintain and enjoy life. Although work is normally considered to be a means to an end, it can also be an enjoyable activity in itself. In fact, because we spend so much of our time working, it is important that it provides some degree of fulfilment. When we are trapped in careers we don't enjoy, or when routine activities become chores, then our quality of life is affected. Because we are all different, we are all naturally attracted to different types of work. However, although it is important to undertake work in accordance with our own nature, it is equally important to believe that the work we do is worthwhile. Nobody enjoys performing tasks they don't believe will benefit themselves or others, but unfortunately, modern society is full of such activities. Humans that live a predominantly natural lifestyle directly experience the benefits of work. For example, hunting and foraging will bring the direct benefit of food, building a simple house will bring the direct benefit of shelter, and practising good hygiene will bring the direct benefit of health. However, although in modern society the division of labour has created greater efficiency, it has also made it difficult to enjoy the benefits of certain types of work. Whilst many jobs are fulfilling, we live in an increasingly mechanised world where millions of jobs are repetitive, mundane tasks that are both soul-destroying and are completely removed from those who benefit from them. Because this mechanistic approach to work often fails to recognise a person's need to be a valued member of society, it can be unrewarding and psychologically damaging.[7]

Recently, there has been a growing trend towards developing nations becoming manufacturing centres for developed ones. Although developed nations have benefited from cheap goods, they have also suffered

---

7 Henry David Thoreau was critical of the division of labour. In *Walden* (published in 1854), he says the labouring man has no time to be anything but a machine. His answer was to live a simpler life of greater self-sufficiency.

from a collapse of their own traditional industries, resulting in unemployment. In addition to this, people in developing nations have had little choice but to work in unpleasant and dangerous conditions just to earn a basic living. This global division of labour has created a world where many countries neglect the work requirements of their own citizens, exploit the poor for cheap products and services, and damage the environment through the unnecessary transportation of goods. It has also created a situation where people often derive little enjoyment from their work because they are detached from its purpose, other than to earn a living. This large-scale division of labour may be an efficient way of producing goods and services, but it has created jobs that are seen as being nothing more than a means to an end.

Because economics largely determines the type of work available to people, not everyone is fortunate enough to be able to choose a career, and many people live in such abject poverty that they will seize any opportunity to earn a living. However, regardless of the type of work we engage in, we should never only view it as a means to an end. All work, regardless of how difficult or mundane it is, should be performed as a service to others. As soon as work is viewed as just a means to gratify one's senses and ego, work loses an important meaning. Therefore, despite our circumstances in life, we should always try to engage in meaningful work that promotes our own wellbeing, benefits others and respects the environment.

**LEISURE**

Our leisure time is important, as not only does it give us the opportunity to relax, but it also gives us the opportunity to enjoy those recreational activities that give meaning to our lives. Although the work we undertake should be enjoyable and meaningful, if we do not utilise our leisure time to enjoy life, then not only may our health suffer, but work also loses much of its purpose. As with all other aspects of life, recreational activities should promote our own wellbeing, respect other living beings and respect the environment; however, the opposite is often the case. The world has become increasingly dominated by Western culture, and too much emphasis is now being placed on gratifying the senses through negative and destructive activities. Many people use their leisure time to watch violent movies, play violent computer games, take recreational drugs, enjoy hobbies that create social isolation, and engage in activities that require little physical effort. Anyone who believes that such activities are conducive to creating a happy life is ignorant of their own fundamental requirements. There is also far too much interest in watching or engaging in competitive sports. Although sport can be something positive that promotes physical and mental wellbeing, when too much emphasis is placed on winning it can have negative consequences. Whilst from a material point of view competition may be desirable, from a spiritual point of view it is not. The desire to win is essentially an expression of the selfish ego, where someone wishes to promote themselves or their team above others. In reality, most competitive sports are probably relatively harmless; however, if the desire to win goes unchecked, it can be psychologically damaging and can also lead to dishonest behaviour.

Unfortunately, modern society has largely shunned the simple pleasures of life, such as having regular meals with family and friends, appreciating art, or enjoying the pleasures of nature, in favour of technology and consumer products. This reliance on technology and manufactured goods to provide entertainment is affecting our physical and mental health, and putting huge pressure on the environment, a situation which is unsustainable. It is also creating people that have an artificial and distorted view of the world, and who are so out of touch with their own basic requirements that they are no longer able to enjoy those things in nature that give meaning and context to their life. As imperfect as this world appears to be, if we have the right attitude to life, we can derive great pleasure from the simplest things. However, this can only be achieved by adopting a more considered and loving approach, becoming fully open to experiencing the present, and appreciating the true beauty of life.

**POLITICS**

Whether we like it or not, politics affects us all. Politics deals with how societies are ordered and governed, and because humans are social animals, it is an inevitable part of life. In fact, because many animals have some kind of social structure, it could be argued that politics is a completely natural expression of all social animals, the only difference with human politics being its complexity. Whilst no political system is perfect, most people recognise the importance of fair governance, and the numerous political ideologies, revolutions and civil wars throughout history are testament to this. However, regardless of how hard humans try to create effective political systems, there will always be situations where even the best ones fail. One of the main reasons for this is that it is extremely difficult to create political systems that respect a person's individual rights, whilst serving the interests of the community. This problem is clearly demonstrated by the opposing systems of capitalism and socialism. Whilst capitalism is an ideology based on individual rights and private ownership, it doesn't adequately address the requirements of society, often resulting in huge inequality and an uneven distribution of wealth. Although socialism addresses many of the problems of capitalism by emphasising greater equality and common ownership, it doesn't adequately recognise the rights and needs of individuals. Also, although socialism can thrive under democratically elected governments, history has shown that it thrives just as well under unelected governments, and can be open to abuse by dictators. Because the rights of individuals and the needs of society are of equal importance, in practice the best political systems are probably ones that have elements of both capitalism and socialism.

Although there are many different forms of government, they all fall into one of two categories – elected and unelected. Whilst democratically elected governments are generally regarded as being the fairest, this does not always mean they are the best. It is true that a democracy most closely reflects the desires of its people, but because many people are neither privy to the kind of information required to make informed political choices, nor possess the understanding required to know what is best for society, democratic governments are rarely any better than the people who elect them. The other problem with democracy is that political parties often put forward policies to satisfy the whims of the majority in order to get elected, rather than create sound but often undesirable policies that are for the greater long-term good of society. Democracy is commonly touted as being a fix for many of the world's political problems; however, if a country doesn't have the right social conditions, political structures and a sufficiently educated populace, then there is every chance democracy will fail. That doesn't mean we should tolerate the abuse and misery that is often inflicted by unelected governments, it just means that good political systems consist of more than democracy alone.

One of the most important features of any good political system is its constitution, as it sets out the beliefs, principles and laws by which a nation is governed. Although many countries have a constitution, they are often ineffective when it comes to the rights of individuals. This is because many constitutions are poorly written, are too complex, or their basic principles are repeatedly ignored. A good constitution is one that puts the rights of individuals, along with respect for other living beings and the environment at its core, and a good government is one that adheres to such a constitution. Any government that allows people to become wealthy at the expense of others, ignores the suffering of other living beings, and allows the unnecessary destruction of the environment to go unchecked, is a government that is fundamentally flawed. Also, any society that freely elects such a government and allows it to flourish is equally as flawed.

Of course, not everyone is fortunate enough to live in a country where they have a say in how it is governed, but those who are should take their democratic responsibilities seriously. It is strange how so many people refrain from voting when they have the opportunity to change things, or repeatedly vote for the same political party simply because they or their family have always voted for them, even though that political party has evolved and its values have completely changed. It is also strange how so many people vote for a political party without truly understanding the implications of its policies, or who are drawn in by election hype and rhetoric. Sometimes, it seems like no political party has much to offer in the way of improving people's lives, but this should not deter us from exercising our right to vote. Whenever we have the opportunity to vote, we should try to be as informed as possible on who or what we are voting for. Also, although we naturally vote for those policies which are likely to benefit us personally, we should place equal importance on voting for policies that will benefit society as a whole. Because we are all dependent on one another, what is beneficial for society is often beneficial for us as individuals. Politics can be complicated, and it is not always clear which policies are best for creating a better society. However, if we are fortunate enough to live in a democracy, and if we understand that happiness is the ultimate goal of life, then providing we make a concerted effort to understand and vote for those policies that are most likely to fulfil this goal, then politically speaking this is as much as can be expected from anyone. And, where we have the desire and opportunity to be a member of a political party or council, then we should take our responsibilities seriously, conduct ourselves with integrity, and always strive to serve the greater good.

Attaining complete life and happiness is ultimately about transcending the egocentric self, and connecting with a higher spiritual dimension through a process of love. This higher spiritual dimension is the very foundation of the universe and the source of all life, and this process of love is the method by which we eradicate the concept of 'I' and achieve greater consciousness. However, we should be careful not to confuse spiritual love with mundane human love. Although human love is also a connecting process, because we are driven by the ego, and because the objects of human love are limited dimensional realities, it is not possible to be completely fulfilled by it. That doesn't mean we should reject the people or things of this world, it just means we should be selective about who or what we connect with. In other words, relative to our situation in life, we should embrace those things that promote greater life and happiness, and reject those things that cause destruction and misery. Because the limited goodness found in this world has its foundations in the absolute goodness of the universe's source, the spiritual process is only ever about pursuing that which is greater. Even from a material point of view, whenever we experience things that give greater fulfillment, then the desire to enjoy those things that are less fulfilling naturally diminishes over time. This is no different to the spiritual point of view. As our conscious life force becomes increasingly transformed by spiritual love, then our desire for material things naturally diminishes, and we also become less affected by negative emotions such as jealousy, hatred and anger. However, if this material world is prematurely rejected out of a belief that it is temporary or illusory, and we do not replace it with a higher spiritual experience, then we will be left feeling empty and frustrated. Therefore, we should see the spiritual path as a process of positive transformation and not a process of rejection.

Contrary to popular belief, spiritual love is not only about giving, but is also about opening ourselves up to receiving. Love is a two-way process, and unless we are open to receiving that which promotes life and happiness, we will not possess the energy to be giving of ourselves in return. Of course, for many people contemplation, meditation and prayer are central to this spiritual process and one should seek guidance on such practices; however, it is important that these practices are also effectively dovetailed with day-to-day living. It is impractical for most people to withdraw from society and become monks, nuns or mendicants, and not everyone wants to follow a religion. Therefore, if we choose to walk this spiritual path, it is important to understand our limits and have a practical approach to life. Although we are all restricted by circumstance, we all have free will. And, whilst the spiritual path is often a difficult one, if we choose to follow it, we will be rewarded with the greatest gift of life and happiness.

In respect of our fifth question 'How should we live?', we can summarise our findings as follows:

**In order to understand how we should live, we must first understand what is success and advancement. Because things such as wealth, status, power, technology and economic growth do not always result in happiness, they are unreliable ways of measuring success and advancement. Instead, because life and happiness is the ultimate goal of life, success and advancement should be measured by this criterion.**

**The body is a reflection of the conditioned conscious life force, and in order to attain complete life and happiness, it requires an inner change away from serving the egocentric self, to one where we put the promotion of life and happiness through a process of love at the heart of everything we do.**

**Although we may come to an intellectual understanding that our conscious life force is eternal, until we transform ourselves spiritually and attain greater life and happiness, we should take a practical approach to the mind and body's requirements.**

By taking a considerate and caring approach to life, we can improve both our physical and spiritual situation. In respect of our own wellbeing, our actions should give personal fulfilment and build physical and mental health. In respect of other living beings, our actions should respect their right to life and should not cause unnecessary suffering. And, in respect of the environment, we should give careful consideration to what impact our actions have on it.

Attaining complete life and happiness is ultimately about transcending the egocentric self, and connecting with a higher spiritual dimension through a process of love. According to our circumstances, we all have the freedom to choose what path we take in life; however, if we choose to follow the spiritual path, we will be rewarded with the greatest gift of life and happiness.